JIST'S PUTTING THE BARS BEHIND YOU SERIES

INSTRUCTOR'S RESOURCE MANUAL

by
Ronald C. Mendlin
and
Marc Polonsky
with **J. Michael Farr**

JIST's Putting the Bars Behind You Series
Instructor's Resource Manual

© 2000 by *Ronald C. Mendlin* and *Marc Polonsky*

Published by JIST Works, an imprint of JIST Publishing, Inc.
8902 Otis Avenue
Indianapolis, IN 46216-1033
Phone: 800-648-JIST   Fax: 800-JIST-FAX   E-Mail: editorial@jist.com

Visit our Web site at http://www.jist.com for more information on JIST, free job search information and book chapters, and to order our many products!

> **This manual has been created especially to be used with the workbooks in JIST's *Putting the Bars Behind You* series:**
>
> *The "Double You": The Person You Are and the Person You Want to Be*
> *Being "Job-Ready": Identify Your Skills, Strengths, and Career Goals*
> *Job Search Tools: Resumes, Applications, and Cover Letters*
> *Networking and Interviewing for Jobs*
> *Keeping Your Job: Survive and Succeed in a New Job*
>
> Four JIST videos make ideal companions for the workbooks in JIST's *Putting the Bars Behind You* series:
>
> *After Prison: How the Ex-Convict Can Find a Place to Live, Get Work, and Stay Straight*
> *Inside Opportunities: Training and Education Behind Bars*
> *Post-Prison Blues: Adjusting Your Relationships with Family, Friends, and Yourself*
> *Putting the Bars Behind You*

Quantity discounts are available for JIST books. Please call our Sales Department at 1-800-648-5478 for a free catalog and more information.

Acquisitions Editor: Michael Cunningham
Development Editor: Sara N. Emmick
Editor: Lori Cates
Copy Editor: Gayle Johnson
Proofreader: Rebecca York
Cover and Interior Designer: Aleata Howard
Page Layout Coordinator: Carolyn J. Newland

Printed in the United States of America

03 02 01 00   9 8 7 6 5 4 3 2 1

ISBN: 1-56370-638-5

Contents

CHAPTER FIVE: Basic Resources for Your Job Search 37

Comprehensive Vocabulary Quiz for Book 1 51

Part II—BEING "JOB-READY": Identify Your Skills, Strengths, and Career Goals   69

CHAPTER ONE: Your Foundation............................71

CHAPTER TWO: Identify Your Experience 75

PART III—JOB SEARCH TOOLS: Resumes, Applications, and Cover Letters   109

Part IV—Networking and Interviewing for Jobs   141

CHAPTER FOUR: During the Interview 163

Comprehensive Vocabulary Quiz for Book 4 176

Part V—Keeping Your Job: Survive and Succeed in a New Job   187

CHAPTER ONE: The Basics 189

CHAPTER TWO: Organize Your Work....................195

CHAPTER THREE: Get Along with Coworkers and Supervisors...201

Introduction

Welcome to JIST's *Putting the Bars Behind You* workbook series. What follows is a summary of the series and its accompanying instructor's manual, as well as the most effective ways to use the materials in your class.

About JIST's *Putting the Bars Behind You* Series

This manual was created especially to accompany JIST's *Putting the Bars Behind You* series. The five workbooks in the series introduce life skills and job search methods in a clear, interactive way.

The techniques presented in JIST's *Putting the Bars Behind You* series work. These methods are based on a total of 60 years of research and helping people find good jobs in less time. Author Ronald Mendlin has placed more than 600 people in jobs, and he knows the challenges that parolees face. Author Mike Farr emphasizes practical, results-oriented methods that put the responsibility for the job search on the student, with extraordinary success.

In the workbooks, students learn basic concepts and then interact with them using worksheets and other special features:

Think About It. Asks the students to apply the concepts they have just read about to their own lives.

Checkpoint. Provides review questions about the text up to that point.

Challenge. Gives the students a chance to put what they've learned into action.

Example. Features words of encouragement and advice from ex-inmates who have faced the same struggles that the students will face.

The workbooks are easy to understand, include many activities, and feature interesting photos and graphics.

Who Is the Putting the Bars Behind You *Series For?*

This series was designed for prison inmates in prerelease and postrelease programs, as well as juvenile offenders in need of career and life guidance. These individuals might have little or no experience with finding work, or it might have been a long time since they last worked or looked for a job.

These workbooks give the students understandable and interesting methods—plus lots of practice—for facing the outside world with confidence. The workbooks present topics in short, digestible sections, using clear, brief sentences. The text is simple enough for anyone with a grade 5 or higher reading level to understand.

If necessary, students can easily work their way through the material without assistance, because the content makes sense on its own. The workbooks give clear directions for each exercise, and each exercise clearly relates to the text that it follows. So if class time is short, you can simply assign a chapter as homework.

How This Manual Is Organized

Each part of this manual covers one workbook in the series. Within each part are several chapters, corresponding to the chapters in the workbooks. Each chapter follows this format:

Chapter Objectives. The objectives of each chapter are stated for your convenience. Present the objectives at the very beginning of the class. This gives focus to the rest of the chapter. You can read these aloud and post them on chart paper, the board, or an overhead projector. When you finish the chapter, refer back to the objectives and ask the students to identify how each one was met. Or, you can check off each objective as you work through the chapter.

Working Vocabulary. Key ideas and new terms are noted at the beginning of each chapter. Present each new word in turn, and have a student read its definition. Post a running list of all the vocabulary words somewhere in the classroom—possibly on the board where it won't be erased, on a piece of chart paper, or on an overhead transparency. You can refer back to the definitions when the class comes across one of these words in the text.

At the conclusion of each workbook, give each student a complete list of the vocabulary words and definitions to keep.

Please note that some students—particularly younger inmates, people who don't speak English well, students with limited reading and writing skills, and students who feel forced to attend the class—might not understand or appreciate the concept of vocabulary words. You can still present the words and definitions orally to these students and reinforce the definitions when the vocabulary words are used in the text.

Presentation Suggestions. These ideas for presenting the material in class save time and help you focus on important concepts. These suggestions are clearly explained, and each suggestion refers to a specific page in the workbooks. The first time you teach the class, you might want to follow all the instructions exactly. As you get more experience, you will figure out which suggestions work best for you, and how to make them fit your teaching style as well as your students' learning styles.

Note: Within these sections you will see references to specific page numbers. If the reference is in parentheses, it refers to a page within this manual. If not, it refers to the corresponding page in the student workbook.

Discussion Questions. These questions can be used to spark class discussion.

Activities. The activities are important practice for working with others in a job setting. This manual presents more activities than you probably will use. This allows you to choose the activities that best fit your time constraints and class dynamics. For example, some classes might work well in small groups, whereas other classes might not be suited to these kinds of activities. (See the later section "Are Small Groups Needed?")

Charts. In many cases, this manual provides examples of charts you can draw on the board or show on an overhead projector to help model the activities or illustrate the topics. Within the text, you will find small pictures of these charts, as well as references to the page numbers of the full-size versions of the charts at the end of the chapter, which you can copy onto transparency sheets for use on an overhead projector.

Checkpoint Answers. This manual provides the answers to the Checkpoint review quizzes in the student workbooks. In some cases, however, the questions will require personal responses that will vary from one student to another.

Think On This.... These sections give students the chance to start thinking about topics that will be covered the next time the class meets. You can ask students to bring written responses to the questions at the next class meeting. If this is not practical, you can ask them to think about the questions until the beginning of the next session. Be sure to address these questions early in the next session, because they are closely linked to the chapter objectives.

Ask the students to guess what the chapter objectives might be based solely on reading the previous **Think On This** assignment. See if the students notice how **Think On This** always gives clues about what they can expect in the next chapter. This works best with the last two or three chapters of each workbook, because by then the students have had some practice.

Comprehensive Quizzes and Answer Keys. Where appropriate, we provide a full-book quiz that you can give students as a review at the end of each workbook. Optionally, you can take these quizzes one step further and tie them in with word puzzles (discussed next) to further reinforce the vocabulary words.

Word Puzzles. Word puzzles have been included to correspond with most chapters in the workbook. These puzzles reinforce the definitions of the **Working Vocabulary** words. You can choose whether or not to use these puzzles with your class, based on their ability to understand and do them. Perhaps you could give the puzzles only to the more literate and motivated students in the class as homework. Or you can choose not to use them at all.

How to Use This Instructor's Resource Manual

This manual makes sense only when used with one or more of the student workbooks. The workbooks are mentioned and referenced by page number and are essential for understanding many of the suggestions and activities.

The workbooks and manual provide a structured curriculum that can be used on an individual basis or in interactive small- and large-group sessions.

The series can be presented as a mini-curriculum within other courses or as a separate, complete job search course. The workbooks can be used separately, as a set, or in any combination you want. The manual and workbooks are all you need to teach basic life and job search skills in the way that works best for you and your students, whatever your time frame or class size may be.

Each workbook and its activities will take an average of 10 to 20 hours of class time to complete. You can expand the course to fit a longer class schedule by encouraging more class discussion, giving students more time to fill out questions and worksheets in the workbooks, using all activities and quizzes, and inviting guest speakers to class. You can adapt the material for a shorter class schedule by skipping some activities or topics, assigning homework, and limiting class discussion.

Materials You Will Need

The following is a list of all the materials you will need during the course of teaching all five workbooks. This includes the materials needed for the **Activity** sections.

- Five two-pocket folders for each student: One red, one green, one blue, one yellow, and one purple. The students will use these folders to store the information they gather during the class. The color of each folder corresponds to the color of the workbook it will be used with.

- A spiral-bound notebook for each student.

- Lined and unlined index cards.

- Lined and unlined 8½ × 11-inch paper.

- Chart paper.

- Pens or pencils.

- Markers.

- Overhead projector, blackboard, or dry-erase board.

- Several blank transparency sheets (if using an overhead projector).

- Popsicle sticks and a cup or jar to keep them in.

- Tape.

- Stapler.

- Scissors (if allowed by prison rules).

- Access to a photocopier.

- Copies of the telephone yellow pages, if allowed. If not allowed, pages photocopied from the yellow pages.

- Envelopes and stamps.

- At least 20 M&Ms of different colors, bingo chips, or anything that can be divided into color groups and separated into percentages.

- Toll-free numbers of job search agencies, as well as any other real examples of job search resources (if allowed).

- Classified ads from several local newspapers, and printouts from several job search Web sites. If these are unavailable or not allowed, mockups may be used.

- Kitchen timer.

- Reference books discussed on page 57 of workbook II.

- Transparency sheets of pages 8–11, 67, 68, 70, 71, 87, 88, 94, and 95 in workbook III.

- A transparency of the JIST Card® on page 42 of workbook IV.

- A phone to use as a prop.

- Pamphlets about sexual harassment to give to the students.

- A book about employment law.

Student Participation

You might find that your students are initially reluctant to participate in the classroom activities. To encourage all students to participate, write each student's name on a Popsicle stick. Place the sticks in a jar or cup. Pull them out one at a time whenever you are in need of a reader or to randomly create small groups.

This manual often tells you to call on students to read parts of the text aloud. Naturally, you can make exceptions for any students who are unable to read. If your class lacks many good readers, you can choose to read the sections aloud yourself.

Small-Group Activities

This manual sometimes suggests that you break your class into small groups to discuss a section or come up with an answer. We do not include activities for small groups in the first workbook because it might take time for you to build the comfort and trust with your class that is needed to make small groups work well. However, group activities can work well in workbooks II through V, provided that you have established the following:

- An explicit contract with students about what they will do in the class, what is expected of them, and what they want to accomplish

- Clearly outlined do's and don'ts for behavior in small groups

- An easy-to-understand, highly structured set of instructions for what the small group needs to accomplish

A Contract with the Students

A sample contract between students and teacher could read as follows:

In taking this prerelease (or postrelease) class, I understand that I am entering into a contract. This contract requires that I

- *Work seriously with the ideas in this class.*

- *Complete the assignments for this class.*

- *Participate in class discussions and activities.*

- *Behave with respect toward myself, the teacher, and my fellow students.*

- *Get past fear and anxiety so that I can learn what I need to learn in this class.*

You can present this contract to the students orally at the beginning of the first class and ask them to agree to it verbally. If you wish, you can also post the contract somewhere in the classroom to remind the students of their mission.

Do's and Don'ts

Do's and don'ts for small-group behavior might include the following:

- Stay on track.
- Don't get involved in conversations unrelated to the task at hand.
- Take turns. Make sure everyone has more or less equal time and contribution to the activity.
- Choose a "representative" to report back to the entire class.
- Choose a small-group "facilitator" to make sure the group is on track and that everyone is giving input.

You should state these do's and don'ts verbally rather than presenting them in a handout, because they might change slightly from activity to activity.

Are Small Groups Needed?

In relatively small classes, such as a dozen or less, you might not need to break into small groups for activities. In bigger classes, such as 20 or more, the small-group activities take on more importance as a way to make sure everyone is involved.

Always be sensitive to the emotional tone of the group you are teaching. Do the students seem comfortable with one another? Is their body language generally tense or fairly relaxed? Do they make eye contact with one another and with you? Do they laugh easily sometimes?

If your students do not seem at least somewhat comfortable, small groups might not be possible for the time being.

Sharing Personal Responses

Be aware that some of your students won't be willing to share their responses to personal questions. They might want to avoid discussing their pasts. In most cases, we have avoided asking for personal information to be shared aloud (although many of the **Think About It** sections ask the students to write their personal responses to questions that require some self-examination).

Other Resource Materials

JIST publishes much material on career and job search topics. One or more of these resources can give you additional information that you might find useful in preparing your presentations.

Workbooks and textbooks. JIST offers a wealth of workbooks and textbooks covering job search topics.

- *Getting the Job You Really Want.* This workbook can be used with or without the instructor's guide. It covers career planning, job seeking, and job survival.

- *Job Survival.* A workbook that teaches the basics of keeping a job once you get it. Also published: an accompanying instructor's guide.

- *Young Person's Occupational Outlook Handbook.* Presents information about 250 jobs from the *OOH* (see below) in simplified form for new readers. Information given for each job includes a job description, needed education and training, projected earnings, job outlook, subjects to study to work toward this job, related jobs, and more.

Reference books. If your students would like more information about what careers are available and the specifics of these kinds of jobs, the following JIST reference books will be helpful to them:

- *America's Top Jobs for People Without a Four-Year Degree.* Features 165 job descriptions for positions that do not require a four-year college degree.

- *Occupational Outlook Handbook.* Contains detailed information about the jobs held by 90 percent of the workforce, including the nature of the work, working conditions, employment outlook, needed qualifications, earnings, and related occupations.

- *O*NET Dictionary of Occupational Titles.* JIST's printed version of the Department of Labor's online employment database. Describes the details of 1,122 jobs, including tasks; earnings; needed education, knowledge, abilities, and skills; general work activities; and job characteristics.

Videos. Videos are an excellent way to add variety to the class routine and supplement the workbooks with different angles on related topics. JIST has created a variety of videos specific to the topics of job search and post-prison transitions:

- *After Prison: How the Ex-Convict Can Find a Place to Live, Get Work, and Stay Straight.* Basic human needs for food, shelter, and employment—critical factors in transition—are the focus of this video. Part of the *Back in the World: Life After Prison* series.

- *Believe in Yourself.* The inspirational story of a motivational speaker who struggled with alcohol abuse and depression. Told in an offbeat, improvisational comedy style that holds viewers' attention.

- *The Complete Job Application.* An entertaining video that highlights the major areas of filling out job applications.

- *Inside Opportunities: Training and Education Behind Bars.* Shows inmates how to take advantage of the education and training opportunities available to them behind bars. Part of the *Back in the World: Life After Prison* series.

- *Positive Feet: Putting Positive Thoughts into Action.* Motivational speaker Byron Ricks makes a convincing argument that positive thinking does not bring its own results—it requires action to make those thoughts reality. Ricks shows his audience how to give their thoughts and goals "positive feet."

- *Post-Prison Blues: Adjusting Your Relationships with Family, Friends, and Yourself.* Former inmates and experts give their valuable insights into how to make the emotional transition between prison and the outside world. Part of the *Back in the World: Life After Prison* series.

- *Putting the Bars Behind You.* Real-life offenders talk about looking for—and finding—jobs. Covers networking, cold-calling, and interviewing, and the unique challenges that ex-offenders face in the job search.

- *Skills Identification.* This award-winning video helps viewers understand what their skills are, identify the hundreds of skills they have, and clarify which skills are most important in the job market.

- *The Two Best Ways to Find a Job.* Covers the techniques that 80 percent of job seekers use to get jobs: networking and cold-calling.

- *Why Should I Hire You?* Learn how to answer the essential question that underlies all job interviews.

Contact JIST for a complete catalog of products, or visit our Web site at www.jist.com. All of the above-mentioned resources and many others are presented in our catalog and on our site.

Good luck to you and your students!

PART I

Instructor's Resources for

THE "DOUBLE YOU":
THE PERSON YOU ARE AND THE PERSON YOU WANT TO BE

WORKBOOK TABLE OF CONTENTS

The "Double You": The Person You Are and the Person You Want to Be

THE "DOUBLE YOU"
THE PERSON YOU ARE AND
THE PERSON YOU WANT TO BE

Ronald L. Mendlin
and Marc Polonsky

jist

Chapter One

The Person You Are

CHAPTER OBJECTIVES

1. To look at the person you are today.

2. To think about what you have learned from your mistakes.

3. To examine your beliefs.

4. To begin to take stock of what you have to offer the world.

5. To look closely at your values and interests.

Working Vocabulary

- **Restructure.** *Restructure* means to organize something differently than it was organized before.

- **Courageous.** Someone who is *courageous* is brave.

- **Responsibility.** Taking *responsibility* means accepting the good or bad outcomes of your actions without blaming someone else.

- **Inspiring.** Anything that's *inspiring* stimulates you and influences you to do something good.

- **Motivated.** When someone is *motivated,* he is willing to do what is necessary to get something done.

- **Value.** A *value* is anything that has personal importance. For example, if getting an education is important to you, that is considered one of your *values.*

- **Fulfill.** To satisfy or live up to what's expected of you.

- **Dedicated.** Being *dedicated* means being committed to a thought, action, idea, or dream.

- **Vocational.** Training that is *vocational* is specific to a particular job.

- **Accomplishment.** An *accomplishment* is anything you've successfully done in the past or will do in the future.

Presentation Suggestions

Begin the class by presenting the **Working Vocabulary** words one at a time on the board/overhead. Be certain that the students understand what each word means. Call on individuals to use the words in sentences or to give a word that means the same thing as each vocabulary word.

Ask the students to follow along as you read the "Who Are You?" section on page 4 of the student workbook. Then ask a student volunteer to read "Mistakes" aloud. Ask the following question:

- *"Do you believe the statement 'He who never makes a mistake never makes anything'? Explain this to me."* (Accept any reasonable answers from the class.)

Ask another student to read the **Example** on pages 4 and 5. Discuss the example briefly, and then ask the class to discuss several ways Jim could possibly have avoided the whole situation. Write these suggestions on the board/overhead. Using the students' suggestions from the board/overhead, start a discussion of other situations during which their suggestions might apply.

Have the students complete "Big Mistakes" on pages 5 and 6 individually. If time allows, have the students write on an index card one mistake they have made recently. Have them add how they happened to make the mistake and, looking back, how they could have avoided the mistake.

Ask a student volunteer to read aloud the top section on page 7: "The World Is on Your Side (Really!)." Stop briefly to review the **Working Vocabulary** words as they appear in the text. Discuss. Ask the following questions:

- *"Why do companies hire ex-offenders?"* (Answer: Because ex-offenders are dedicated and motivated.)

- *"What reasons might they have for not wanting everybody to know this fact?"* (Answer: It might turn off or frighten customers and coworkers.)

- *"Can this fact help you? In what ways?"* (Answer: Yes. People you work with will not know your past. You will have a fresh start.)

Instruct the students to read the **Example** at the bottom of page 7 silently. Follow this by having them do **Activity #1** if you have time and if you think your students will be able to do it (see page 42).

Have the students complete **Think About It** on page 8 individually.

Give the students time to read page 9 silently. When they are finished, draw the following diagram on the board/overhead (see page 55 for a transparency master of this diagram):

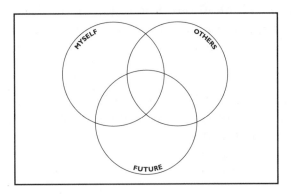

Be sure to draw the diagram large enough so that you can write big enough to make it easy for the students to read. Ask the students to give three beliefs about themselves. Write these in the MYSELF section. Ask for three beliefs about others and write these in the OTHERS section. Then ask for three beliefs about the future and write these in the FUTURE section. Keep this on the board/overhead while the students complete **Think About It** on pages 10–12. Tell them they have to use different examples than the ones on the board.

Ask a student to read aloud "What You Have to Offer" on page 13. Then give each student a copy of the following chart (see page 56 for a full-sized version that you can photocopy):

SCHOOL SKILLS	WORK SKILLS	LEISURE SKILLS

Ask another student to read aloud "Accomplishments and Strengths" on page 13. Tell the students to look at the chart and **Think About It** on pages 13–14. Have the students complete **Think About It** first. Then have them break down their skills using the categories from the chart. Have the students put the completed chart in their **red folders** (these folders are discussed in the **Introduction**).

Review with your students the terms *value, responsibility,* and *fulfill* from the **Working Vocabulary.** Move directly on to complete pages 14–19. Read each question aloud to the students and have them write their responses. Help students individually if they need help.

Have students complete **Think About It** on page 19 individually. Then ask them to copy the three most important things they have to offer the world onto the front of their **red folders.** (Example: I can offer _____ , _____ , and _____ to the world.)

Complete **Checkpoint** on page 20. Responses will vary from student to student. If you have time, give the students some time to write or think on their own about the topics discussed in the classroom that day.

Quick Quiz

Name: _____

Directions: *Find and circle the vocabulary words in the following puzzle.*

A	C	C	O	M	P	L	I	S	H	M	E	N	T	U
R	O	Y	Y	D	S	P	H	Z	V	E	R	S	I	S
L	E	P	C	O	U	R	A	G	E	O	U	S	X	A
Z	A	S	T	D	C	T	K	C	K	C	T	M	E	U
B	T	H	P	L	A	N	O	I	T	A	C	O	V	P
J	V	P	M	O	O	C	J	J	B	D	U	T	A	J
U	R	D	Z	A	N	V	G	I	E	E	R	I	L	N
D	I	Q	I	I	C	S	N	D	I	D	T	V	U	E
L	E	U	F	U	L	F	I	L	L	T	S	A	E	Z
I	W	V	H	N	M	C	R	B	A	W	E	T	V	L
W	E	W	C	X	A	L	I	C	I	U	R	E	Q	T
G	C	H	C	T	L	O	P	N	B	L	T	D	V	P
O	H	W	E	L	O	M	S	A	S	V	I	F	H	C
F	N	D	S	C	Y	N	N	L	Z	U	Q	T	C	B
F	D	C	D	A	O	P	I	U	Y	T	A	Z	Y	Y

Accomplishment

Courageous

Dedicated

Fulfill

Inspiring

Motivated

Responsibility

Restructure

Value

Vocational

Quick Quiz Answer Key

A	C	C	O	M	P	L	I	S	H	M	E	N	T	U
R	O	Y	Y	D	S	P	H	Z	V	E	R	S	I	S
L	E	P	C	O	U	R	A	G	E	O	U	S	X	A
Z	A	S	T	D	C	T	K	C	K	C	T	M	E	U
B	T	H	P	L	A	N	O	I	T	A	C	O	V	P
J	V	P	M	O	O	C	J	J	B	D	U	T	A	J
U	R	D	Z	A	N	V	G	I	E	E	R	I	L	N
D	I	Q	I	I	C	S	N	D	I	D	T	V	U	E
L	E	U	F	U	L	F	I	L	L	T	S	A	E	Z
I	W	V	H	N	M	C	R	B	A	W	E	T	V	L
W	E	W	C	X	A	L	I	C	I	U	R	E	Q	T
G	C	H	C	T	L	O	P	N	B	L	T	D	V	P
O	H	W	E	L	O	M	S	A	S	V	I	F	H	C
F	N	D	S	C	Y	N	N	L	Z	U	Q	T	C	B
F	D	C	D	A	O	P	U	U	Y	T	A	Z	Y	Y

Think On This...

- What are some of the dreams you once had for the future?

- Who did those dreams include?

- Have you taken any steps toward fulfilling those dreams, or have you changed them?

- If someone asked you to write down your life's goal today, what would it be?

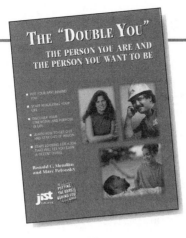

Chapter Two

The Person You Want to Be

CHAPTER OBJECTIVES

1. To think about the people you need to reconnect with, forgive, and avoid.

2. To reflect on your dreams and desires.

3. To start setting short-term and long-term goals for yourself.

4. To write a personal mission statement.

Working Vocabulary

- **Goals.** *Goals* are something to work toward achieving, something that you want for yourself.

- **Personal mission statement.** A *personal mission statement* is a paragraph (or paragraphs) that contains your goals in life and what you believe in.

- **Reestablish.** To *reestablish* means to rebuild, but stronger than before.

- **Forgiveness.** When there is no more fault or blame, there is *forgiveness.*

- **Confront.** When people come face to face to talk about something, they *confront* one another.

Presentation Suggestions

Note: This chapter requires some deep thinking from the students. Take it slowly and give the students individual help if they need it.

Begin the class by posting the **Chapter Objectives** on the board/ overhead. Next, reread **Think On This...** from the end of chapter 1 of this resource manual. Discuss the students' responses and how they relate to the chapter 2 objectives.

Then add the **Working Vocabulary** words for chapter 2 to the list from the first chapter. Read the word and definition for each word, and then choose five students to read each of the words out loud to the class.

Read the "Rebuilding Bridges" section on page 22 aloud to the class. Ask the following question:

- *"Why do you think it's a good idea to reestablish relationships by writing letters first?"* (Answer: Accept all reasonable responses. Here are some examples: Writing letters is nonthreatening and lets you share your feelings without fear of a confrontation. It also gives each person time to heal.)

Give the students time to complete the two-column table on page 22, listing who they will write letters to and what they will tell these people.

Call on a student to read aloud the first three paragraphs of "Forgiveness" on page 23. Write the quote from Archbishop Tutu on the board/overhead. Ask the students to copy the quote onto the front of their **red folders** in bold print. Continue reading, calling on a second student to read the next two paragraphs and a third student to read the final paragraph. Draw the following diagram on the board/overhead (see page 57 for a transparency master of this diagram):

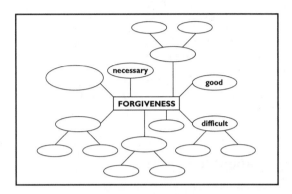

Give each student a blank sheet of paper to copy the diagram onto. Ask the students to say any word that they think is related to forgiveness. Write these words on the board or overhead, surrounding the main word and connecting to it. Accept as many responses as you have time for. If the students can't come up with enough responses on their own, here are some examples you could give them to help them get going:

- Necessary
- Patient
- Good
- Difficult

- Church
- Quiet
- Personal

Have the students place their diagrams in their **red folders** when they are done with them. Then give the students time to complete the chart on page 23. The chart is about people they need to forgive and be forgiven by.

Ask a student volunteer to read aloud "The People You Should Avoid" on page 24. Discuss the questions in the paragraph with the group. Be aware that some students won't want to discuss their personal answers to these questions, so don't pressure people to name names out loud. They can save their answers for **Think About It** on page 25.

Use the following diagram as a guide for the board or overhead display to use as you begin and continue this discussion (see page 58 for a transparency master):

AVOID OR ACCEPT

- **WHICH PEOPLE OR PLACES CAN MAKE YOUR LIFE BETTER?**

- **WHICH PEOPLE OR PLACES WERE PART OF THE PROBLEM?**

- **HOW CAN YOU BE SURE TO MAKE A NEW START? WHAT IS YOUR PLAN?**

Have a student read aloud the **Example** at the bottom of page 24. Then have the students complete **Think About It** on page 25.

Ask the students to read the bottom of page 25, "Dreams and Desires," silently. Discuss the idea of an obituary—the story in the newspaper about a person who has died, which lists the person's accomplishments and relatives. Ask the following question:

● *"Why do people write obituaries for people who have died?"* (Answer: It is a way of remembering loved ones and their lives.)

Give each student a half sheet of lined paper. Tell them to write their name centered at the top of the first line. On the second line, have them write the year of their birth below their name. Tell them not to fill in the year of death, but to put a "?" there.

Then give the students time to write their own obituaries as they would like them to read sometime in the future. Remind them that obituaries usually list the deceased person's accomplishments throughout their life, as well as their family members. The students may read these out loud as they finish. Have them place the obituaries in their **red folders.**

Call on a student to read aloud "Productive Daydreaming" on page 26. Be prepared for some students to react doubtfully about this concept. Tell them that although it sounds funny, everybody has done it at one time, and it works.

Then have the students complete **Think About It** on pages 26–27.

Ask another student to read aloud "Reasonable Expectations" on page 27. Follow with **Activity #2** (see page 43).

Have the students read "Life Goals" on pages 27–28 silently. Then have the students complete the **Goals Worksheets** on pages 28–29.

Tell the students, "Close your eyes. Relax. Imagine you have been released from prison and things are going just like you hoped. What are you doing? Where are you living? Who are the people in your life? What kind of job do you have? Think about these things until I tell you to open your eyes."

Wait about two minutes. Then say, "I am going to give you a sheet of paper. I want you to open your eyes and do one of two things. Draw a picture of your life in the future that shows all the things you thought of, or write a paragraph or two that tells about your life in the future. Take your time." You may need to help and guide some of the students.

When the students are done with their drawing and writing, read aloud the text at the bottom of page 29, "Goal Questions Worksheet," to the students. Have the students begin filling out this worksheet by choosing three to six short-term and long-term goals for their lives. When they are done choosing their goals, help them answer each of the four questions for each goal.

Review the definition of *mission statement.* Ask a student to read the first two paragraphs on page 33. You will read the sample mission statement to the students. It might be helpful to copy the mission statement onto a transparency sheet to help focus the students' attention.

The class may finish reading pages 33–34 silently. Point out the use of the phrase "I will..." as a statement of confidence that what is stated will become reality. Complete **Challenge** on page 34. Give each student a sheet of lined paper to copy and revise their mission statements. Have the students put this in their **red folders** when they are done.

Have the students complete **Checkpoint** on page 35–36. (Answers will vary based on the personal experiences of the students.)

This was a very long and difficult chapter for the students. When they have finished this chapter, find some way to reward them and show them that they have accomplished something big. This will give them something to celebrate before they begin the next chapter.

Quick Quiz

Name: _____

Directions: *Complete the following crossword puzzle. The answers to the puzzle are all vocabulary words from chapters 1 and 2.*

Across

1. To meet face-to-face

6. What you work toward

7. What you have done well

8. Something important to you

9. Job-specific training

Down

2. Important thing you have to do

3. Pardoning someone

4. Put something in a new order

5. To build again

Quick Quiz Answer Key

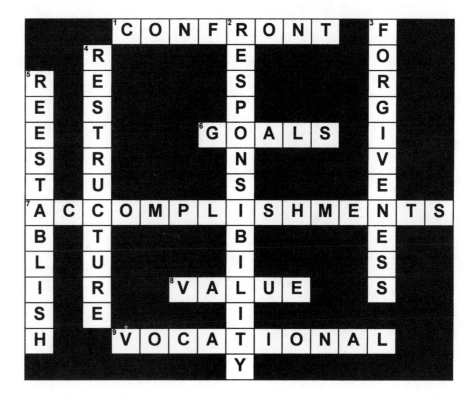

The completed crossword puzzle contains the following answers:

1. CONFRONT
2. RESPONSIBILITY
3. FORGIVENESS
4. RESTRUCTURE
5. REESTABLISH
6. GOALS
7. ACCOMPLISHMENTS
8. VALUE
9. VOCATIONAL

Think On This...

- What do you really think of the world outside of prison?

- Are you prepared to find help if you need it?

- Have you thought about a plan to build positive relationships, communications, and skills?

- Is your plan realistic?

- What does it involve? Describe your world and your plan.

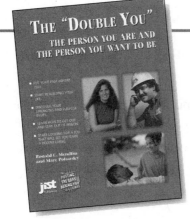

THE "DOUBLE YOU"
THE PERSON YOU ARE AND
THE PERSON YOU WANT TO BE

Chapter Three

Life Skills— When You Get Out of Prison

CHAPTER OBJECTIVES

1. To develop a positive attitude for life in the outside world.

2. To look at your basic needs and learn where to find help.

3. To keep in mind the importance of staying clean and sober.

4. To prepare to deal with difficult emotions.

5. To develop communication, conflict-resolution, and listening skills.

6. To think about money management.

7. To plan time-management strategies.

Working Vocabulary

- **Conflict resolution.** Solving a problem without being violent is using *conflict resolution*.

- **Communication.** Listening to and understanding another person, and talking so that the other person understands you, is *communication*.

- **Attitude.** Personal feelings that other people can guess without hearing you speak, is *attitude*.

- **Paranoia.** *Paranoia* is looking at the world negatively and suspiciously, thinking that everyone is against you.

- **Community.** The people and places that are around someone most often are his or her *community*.

- **Compromise.** When each person in a conflict gives up something and gets something in return, there is a *compromise*.

- **Collaboration.** Working together and sharing ideas is *collaboration*.

- **Expenses.** Things on which you must spend money, such as food, clothing, and a place to live, are *expenses*.

Presentation Suggestions

Read the **Chapter Objectives** to the class. Add new vocabulary words to the list on the board or overhead. Reread **Think On This...** from chapter 2. Discuss the students' responses to these questions as a group.

Ask a student to read aloud "Attitude" and the **Example** on page 38. Ask the class to give examples of the ways other people can pick up on your attitude even if you don't say a word.

Then have the students read "The Outside Is Different" and the following **Example** on pages 38–39 silently. Discuss the sections using the board/overhead display on the following page (see page 59 for a transparency master):

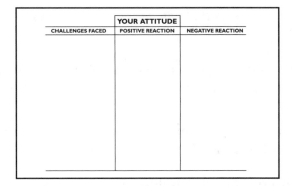

	YOUR ATTITUDE	
CHALLENGES FACED	POSITIVE REACTION	NEGATIVE REACTION

Ask the students to list as many challenges toward attitude as they can find in the text on pages 38–39, including both **Examples.** Then ask them to give an example of a negative reaction to the challenge and a positive reaction to the challenge. Then ask them to think of some challenges they will face on their own when they get out of prison. List these in the chart as well. Be sure to emphasize the benefits of having a positive attitude.

Next, have the students complete **Think About It** on pages 39–41.

Read "Keeping a Positive Attitude" on page 41 aloud to the class. Write the following on the board/overhead in bold letters:

K. F. LAB (Write it like a name that is abbreviated, like "Roy G. Biv.")

Give each student one index card and instruct them to write these letters on the card. On the back of the card, they will write the meanings associated with the initials:

K	Keep **kind** thoughts.
F	Envision **future** successes.
L	Remember what you've **learned.**
A	Emphasize your **accomplishments.**
B	Stay very **busy.**

Underneath the K.F. LAB, write SPECIALIZING IN SUCCESS STORIES! on both the board/overhead and the index cards. Tell the students that they can look at this card whenever they think they have a bad attitude and want to work toward having a good attitude. Have the students put these index cards in their **red folders.**

Choose a student to read aloud the "Choices" section on pages 41–42. Discuss briefly. Ask the questions on the following page.

- *"What are some ways that you decide which choices to make?"* (Answers will vary.)

- *"What are some ways you will improve how you will make decisions in the future?"* (Answers will vary.)

Then have the students answer the questions in **Think About It** on pages 42–43. Follow with **Activity #3** (see page 44).

Ask a student to read aloud the "Survival Needs" section on pages 43–44. Have the student, or a second student, continue reading aloud "Finding Help" on pages 44–45. As the student reads out loud each place to find help, list them on the board/overhead. Give the students paper to write down each help source and what it might give them. Have the students put the completed list in their **red folders.** You could also tell them to write the list on the back of their folders so that they can find it easily later.

Have a student read aloud the part of Reggie in the **Example** on page 45. Then have the students complete **Think About It** on pages 45–46.

Ask the class to read "Clean and Sober" on page 47 silently. When the group has finished, ask the following questions and have the students give their answers out loud:

- *"Why is staying clean and sober so important?"* (Answer: Alcohol and drugs change the way your mind thinks and make it hard to behave the right way.)

- *"What is necessary to stop yourself from using or drinking?"* (Answer: Self-control.)

- *"Describe the cycle that gets people into trouble."* (Answer: Problems cause people to use drugs or drink, and then the using and drinking cause even more problems.)

- *"Which agencies offer 12-step programs?"* (Answers: Alcoholics Anonymous and Narcotics Anonymous.)

- *"What are two benefits of going to the 12-step meetings?"* (Answers: Spiritual and emotional support; staying clean and sober; a chance to tell your story; a place to make friends.)

After you discuss the answers to the questions, ask a student to read aloud "Get a Sponsor!" on pages 47–48. Then have the class read "Fear and Confusion" on pages 48–49 silently. When the group has finished reading, ask the students the following questions:

- *"Do you agree with what this section says? Why or why not?"*

- *"Where will you spend your time when you are released from prison?"*

- *"What kinds of situations might make you feel fearful or confused?"*

- *"How will you react to these situations?"*

Use these questions to start a discussion.

Then call on a student to read aloud the **Example** on page 49.

Ask the following questions:

- *"How did George keep from following his bad impulses?"* (Answer: Buying cassettes.)

- *"What do you think you could use to keep yourself from following your bad impulses?"* (Accept any and all appropriate responses.)

It might be helpful to write these suggestions on the board/overhead. Suggest that the students write the ones they think will work for them on an inside pocket of the **red folder.**

Have the students complete **Think About It** on pages 50–51.

Ask a student to read aloud "Community" on pages 51–52. Assign **Think About It** on page 52 as homework.

Review the definitions of both *communication* and *conflict resolution*. Ask a student to read aloud "Communication" on page 53. After the student finishes reading "Communication," use the following diagram on the board/overhead to expand the discussion (see page 60 for a transparency master):

SITUATION	TYPES OF COMMUNICATION	
	VISUAL (BODY)	VERBAL
1) CLERK APPEARS TO STARE AT YOU.		
2) SOMEONE ASKS WHERE YOU'RE FROM.		
3) YOU ARE ASKED IF YOU HAVE TRANSPORTATION.		
4) SOMEONE BUMPS INTO YOU IN A STORE.		
5) A CUSTOMER ASKS IF YOU HAVE SEEN THEIR KEYS.		

Read the first situation from the top of the left column and call on a volunteer to act out a verbal response and a visual response. Emphasize positive, nonthreatening reactions. Then write a summary of the student's actions under VERBAL and VISUAL on the board/overhead. Have a little fun with this exercise!

Write RESOLVING CONFLICTS on the board/overhead, and then write the headings from the following diagram (see page 61 for a transparency master):

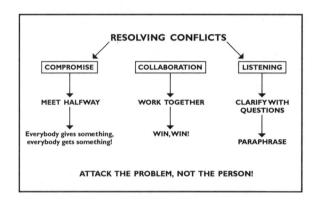

RESOLVING CONFLICTS

COMPROMISE	COLLABORATION	LISTENING
MEET HALFWAY	WORK TOGETHER	CLARIFY WITH QUESTIONS
Everybody gives something, everybody gets something!	WIN, WIN!	PARAPHRASE

ATTACK THE PROBLEM, NOT THE PERSON!

Have the students read silently the sections on pages 53–57. Allow 3–5 minutes per section. Begin a discussion based on the assigned readings to make sure the students understand the sections. After each section is read, stop and add the details under the arrows. Ask the students to come up with their own details, and add these to the board/overhead display. This is only a guide for a board/overhead display; it can be changed or expanded based on class input.

Ask the students to write the phrase from the bottom of the diagram ("Attack the problem, not the person!") somewhere on their **red folders.**

Have the students complete **Checkpoint** on pages 57–58. Then review the answers together as a group.

Checkpoint Answers

1. Compromise and collaboration.

2. Living with others; dealing with less structure. (Uses of strategies will vary based on the students' experiences.)

3. Making questions clear; repeating what the other person said using different words; using phrases such as "Do you think..." and "Do you mean...".

4. Answers will vary.

Call on a student to read aloud "Money Matters: Managing Your Finances" and "Two Important Fixed Expenses." Tell the class that you will give an example of an expense. Ask them to identify it as fixed, variable, or periodic.

EXAMPLES:

Rent (fixed)

Cheaper car that you can pay for in cash (periodic)

New car that you have to get a loan for (fixed)

Restaurant (variable)

New suit (periodic)

House loan payment (fixed)

Water bill (variable)

Medical bills (periodic)

Christmas gifts (periodic)

Next, have the students complete **Think About It** on page 60.

Call on a student to read aloud "Getting Credit" on page 61. Ask the following question:

- *"What is the most important thing to do with your credit card debt at the end of every month?"* (Answer: Pay off the balance completely.)

Ask a student to read aloud the directions for the **Time-Tracking Worksheet.** Be sure the class understands all the instructions. Discuss the difference between productive time and leisure (fun) time.

You can have the students complete the worksheets during the next class session. Or have the students put these pages in their **red folders** and complete them after they get out of prison. Or you can give students two copies of these pages: one set to complete now and another to complete later, after they are out of prison.

If you choose to do this exercise now, have the students complete **Think About It** on pages 65–66 during the next class session.

Follow with **Activity #4** if your class can do it (see page 46).

Choose several students to read aloud the sections on pages 67–68. Then have the students complete **Think About It** on page 68.

Praise the students for their efforts in working through this chapter. It is a very serious subject, and the students will recognize that fact.

Quick Quiz

Name: _____

Directions: *Find and circle the chapter 3 vocabulary words in this puzzle.*

C	O	M	M	U	N	I	C	A	T	I	O	N	V	N
O	O	C	O	C	Z	A	A	D	C	C	O	O	I	R
L	S	M	A	M	O	X	O	M	U	I	K	U	E	T
L	V	S	P	R	Y	M	T	J	Y	V	R	Q	J	U
A	Z	B	N	R	S	G	M	G	P	X	N	B	H	L
B	I	Z	X	N	O	I	T	U	L	O	S	E	R	A
O	P	X	T	J	S	M	E	J	N	P	Z	E	W	F
R	T	I	C	D	W	X	I	T	J	I	X	V	A	G
A	T	T	I	T	U	D	E	S	Y	P	T	Y	S	G
T	Q	F	L	G	F	Y	W	B	E	E	T	Y	M	I
I	A	B	F	P	A	R	A	N	O	I	A	S	P	B
O	R	V	N	J	F	R	S	P	U	K	Z	X	P	L
N	F	U	O	X	M	E	A	C	S	I	S	X	Z	X
B	H	C	C	Z	S	V	C	G	N	F	E	V	X	C

Attitude   Community   Conflict   Paranoia

Collaboration   Compromise   Expenses   Resolution

Quick Quiz Answer Key

```
C O M M U N I C A T I O N V N
O O C O C Z A A D C C O O I R
L S M A M O X O M U I K U E T
L V S P R Y M T J Y V R Q J U
A Z B N R S G M G P X N B H L
B I Z X N O I T U L O S E R A
O P X T J S M E J N P Z E W F
R T I C D W X I T J I X V A G
A T T I T U D E S Y P T Y S G
T Q F L G F Y W B E E T Y M I
I A B F P A R A N O I A S P B
O R V N J F R S P U K Z X P L
N F U O X M E A C S I S X Z X
B H C C Z S V C G N F E V X C
```

Think On This...

- Now that you know how to keep a positive attitude, how can you apply this to a job search?

- What will you say when a potential employer asks about your past?

- Will you be able to face that question with confidence?

- Who did you choose to ask for help in the exercise on page 52?

- What information did they give you?

- Where will you keep this information so that you will have it when you are on your own?

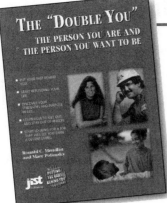

Chapter Four

Job Search Preparation

CHAPTER OBJECTIVES

1. To develop a positive job search attitude.

2. To face the challenges of ex-offender status and establish self-trust.

3. To develop persistence, confidence, and enthusiasm.

4. To overcome fear, discouragement, procrastination, and rejection.

5. To remember to reward and take care of yourself.

Working Vocabulary

- **Persistence.** Trying again over and over and not giving up shows *persistence.*

- **Procrastination.** *Procrastination* is when you put something off until the last minute.

- **Self-esteem.** The way people feel about themselves is their *self-esteem.*

- **Enthusiasm.** Excitement and energy about someone or something is *enthusiasm.*

- **Sincerity.** Being truthful and honest, and meaning what you say, are signs of *sincerity.*

- **Interview.** An *interview* is a meeting with a potential employer to discuss your qualifications for a job.

- **Trait.** A *trait* is a part of your personality.

Presentation Suggestions

Discuss **Think On This...** from the end of chapter 3. Ask the students to try to guess at least three objectives for chapter 4 based on the **Think On This...** questions. Write these on the board/overhead and then give the students the actual objectives. See how close the students' guesses were to the actual objectives.

Read the **Working Vocabulary** to the students and add it to the previous lists. Be sure to review the definitions when the words appear in the text. Do this for both the old and new vocabulary words.

Ask the following question:

- *"Who remembers what was discussed about attitude in chapter 3?"* (Answer: Stay positive; people can sense good or bad attitudes; good attitudes get you much further than bad attitudes.)

Use this question as an introduction to having a student read aloud "Attitude" on page 70.

Then have the students complete **Think About It** on page 70 and the **Daily Planner Worksheet** on page 71. Have the students pull out page 71 and put it in their **red folders**. Follow this with **Activity #5** if you choose (see page 47).

Choose several students to read aloud "The Challenges of Being an Ex-Offender" on page 72, one section at a time. Allow time for discussion.

Ask two students to volunteer for short role-playing exercises. Give each student a slip of paper: one with the word CONFIDENT written on it and the other with the word UNSURE written on it. Ask interview-type questions. Each student should answer in a way that goes along with his or her attitude slip. Next, ask the class to contrast the two interviewees, telling how they were different from each other. Write their responses on the board/overhead in two columns, one for each student. Use the following diagram for the board display (see page 62 for a transparency master):

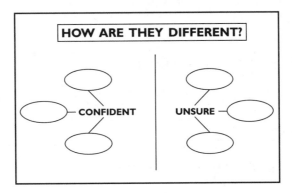

Have the students complete **Think About It** on page 73.

Choose a student to read the first five paragraphs of "The Job of Getting a Job" on page 74. Ask the following question:

● *"How many hours a week should you spend on job hunting?"* (Answer: 38.)

Allow time for the students to write SPEND 38 HOURS A WEEK LOOKING FOR A JOB somewhere on their **red folders**.

Choose two students to read the dialogue and the responses on pages 74–75. Using two different voices often makes students pay more attention. After reading these sections, discuss them as a class.

Assign the "Persistence" section on pages 75–76 to be read silently. When the students have finished reading, ask the following questions:

- *"Who can give an example of someone they know personally or someone famous who has shown persistence?"* (Answers will vary.)

- *"How did they keep going, against the odds?"* (Answers: Accept all reasonable responses.)

Write some of the names on the board/overhead.

Select several students to read aloud sections of "Overcoming Fear, Procrastination, Rejection, and Discouragement" on pages 76–77. Ask the following questions:

- *"When should you reward yourself?"* (Answer: After finishing what you promised yourself you would do.)

- *"How many times are people told 'no' before they get a 'yes'?"* (Answer: At least five, if not more.)

Follow with **Activity #6** if appropriate (see page 48).

Ask the students to silently read "Who Can I Ask?" on page 77. Then have them complete the list on page 78 by themselves. Have the students tear out page 78 and put it in their **red folders.**

Choose students to read aloud the sections on page 79 and the top of page 80. Ask the following questions:

- *"What is the biggest advantage college graduates have over other people?"* (Answer: They think "rich.")

- *"What does GED stand for and what does it take the place of?"* (Answers: Graduate Equivalency Diploma; a high school diploma.)

- *"What can make or break someone who is interviewing for a job besides their qualifications?"* (Answer: personality or attitude.)

Select a student to read aloud the "Enthusiasm" section on pages 80–81. Explain what each of the positive qualities listed on page 80 means.

Assign "Generating Enthusiasm" on page 81 to be read silently. Then have the students complete **Think About It** on pages 82–83. Suggest they write the word ENTHUSIASM on their **red folders**, surrounded by ways to stay enthusiastic.

Assign "Generating Confidence" on page 84 to be read silently. Then have the students complete **Think About It** on pages 85–86. When everyone has finished, have the students take out their notebook journals and write down anything that they feel they have learned about their own confidence. Tell them to write about how they would like to be able to view the world when they are released. Suggest that they write the word CONFIDENCE on their **red folders**, surrounded by ways to maintain it.

Ask a student to read "Take Care of Yourself" on pages 87–88 aloud.

Ask the students to complete **Checkpoint** on pages 88–89. Give the correct answers in class and discuss them with the students.

Checkpoint Answers

1. Attitude, confidence, commitment, setting goals.

2. You can overcome ex-offender challenges by convincing potential employers that they can trust you and by trusting yourself.

3. 38 hours per week.

4. The real reason most people are hired is their personality.

5. Answers will vary.

Quick Quiz

Name: _____

Directions: *Complete the following crossword puzzle.*
The answers are vocabulary words from chapters 3 and 4.

Across

2. Working together

4. Meet halfway

6. Extreme distrust

7. Putting off until later

8. The way you feel; it's obvious to other people

9. Meaning what you say

10. Bills, rent, etc.

Down

1. Speaking to be understood and hearing what is said

3. Meeting with an employer to talk about a job

5. Trying again and again

Quick Quiz Answer Key

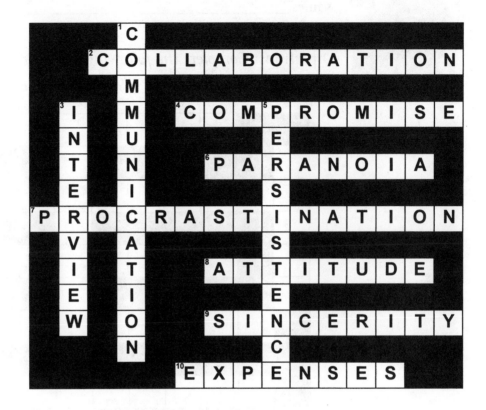

Quick Quiz

Name: _____

Directions: *Complete the following crossword puzzle.*
The answers are vocabulary words from chapters 3 and 4.

Across

1. Feelings of self-worth

4. Solving a problem

5. The people in your life

6. A disagreement

7. Need money for these

Down

2. Excitement or energy

3. Part of your personality

Quick Quiz Answer Key

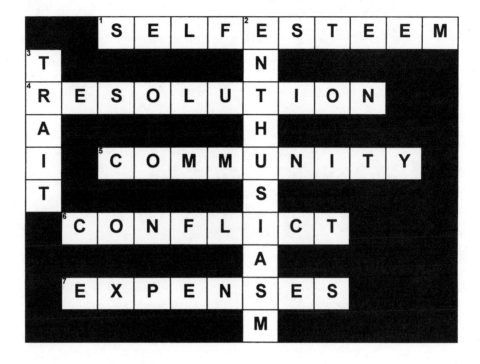

The crossword puzzle solution:

- 1 (Across): SELF ESTEEM
- 2 (Down): ENTHUSIASM
- 3 (Down): TRAIT
- 4 (Across): RESOLUTION
- 5 (Across): COMMUNITY
- 6 (Across): CONFLICT
- 7 (Across): EXPENSES

Think On This...

Your confidence is high! Your enthusiasm is high! Now go find a job! But wait:

- Who do you go to?

- Where do you begin?

- Have you thought of an action plan?

Begin by coming up with three places to look for job openings. In your head, put a star next to the one you think is your best option, at least right now.

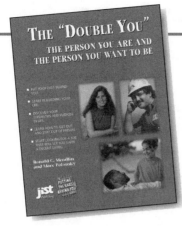

Chapter Five

Basic Resources for Your Job Search

CHAPTER OBJECTIVES

1. To get an overview of places to learn about job openings.

2. To think about which employment resources might be the most valuable.

3. To learn the best ways to respond to job postings.

Working Vocabulary

- **Resource.** A *resource* is any place, person, or thing that gives information or assistance.

- **Job market.** The *job market* is not a specific place to find job openings. It's the total number of jobs that are available in your area or field.

- **Hidden job market.** The *hidden job market* refers to job openings that are not advertised, that you can find out about by just talking to people.

- **Career counselor.** A *career counselor* is someone who helps people find out what their interests and job goals are and helps them find the right job.

- **Apprentice.** An *apprentice* learns a trade through on-the-job experience with limited classroom instruction.

Presentation Suggestions

Discuss the **Think On This...** questions from the end of chapter 4. Write some of the students' thoughts on the board/overhead. Leave these on the board as you introduce the **Chapter Objectives** for chapter 5. Ask the students to identify the similarities between the **Think On This...** topic and chapter 5's objectives.

Introduce chapter 5's **Working Vocabulary**, adding the words to the previous lists of vocabulary words. Review all vocabulary words from chapters 1 through 5. Give the students a test on the vocabulary words for the whole book. The **Comprehensive Vocabulary Quiz for Book 1** is at the end of this chapter (see page 51).

Choose a student to read aloud "Introduction: What You Can Expect from These Resources" on page 92. Follow it with **Activity #7** if appropriate (see page 49).

Before asking a student to read aloud the "Job and Career Counseling Centers" and "'Temp' Agencies" sections on pages 92–93, give each student or pair of students a copy of the local yellow pages. As a student reads this section aloud, the rest of the class can look up these areas and choose examples to share out loud. (If your students are not allowed to have copies of the yellow pages, use a mock-up or skip this activity.)

Review the definition of *apprentice* and then call on a student to read aloud "Apprenticeship Programs" on page 93. Give the students paper, envelopes, and stamps. Allow 10–15 minutes for the students to write a brief letter requesting information from the Department of Labor about a particular apprenticeship program. Have the students address and stamp the envelopes. After class, mail the letters for the students.

Choose two students to read aloud "Employment Agencies" and "The State Employment Development Department" on page 94. Use the following board/overhead display to show the differences between the two types of agencies (see page 63 for a transparency master):

EMPLOYMENT AGENCIES

GOVERNMENT
- No fee.
- Also called the "Unemployment Office."
- Employers are able to list job openings there. If you are qualified for a certain job, the office will send you on an interview.
- Only 5 percent of job seekers find jobs through this service.

PRIVATE
- Charge a fee; sometimes paid by the hiring employer.
- You may have to pay a percentage of your first year's wages if you're hired through an agency.
- Although agencies place want ads for openings they know about, jobs are often gone very quickly.
- 5 percent of job seekers find work this way.
- How they work: The agency calls employers to find out about job openings, then matches the openings with qualified registered people.

Give each student two 3 × 5 index cards to copy the main points of the information and place it in their **red folders.**

The idea of percentages is difficult for some people to understand, so it might be helpful to ask 5 percent of the class to stand up (one student out of every 20 students), to give the class a visual example. If there are fewer than 20 students in the class, use M&Ms of different colors, bingo chips, or anything else that can be divided into color groups and separated into percentages. You will need at least 20 objects for the percentages to work out evenly.

Ask the students the following questions:

- *"Which type of agency is sometimes called the Unemployment Office?"* (Answer: Government.)

- *"Which type of agency charges a fee for its services?"* (Answer: Private.)

- *"How does a private agency usually collect its fee?"* (Answer: It takes a percentage of your salary from your new job.)

Choose one student to read aloud both "Job Hot Lines" and "Classified Ads" on pages 94–95. Write a list of job search resources on the board/overhead. Use the following diagram for the suggested board display (see page 64 for a transparency master):

JOB SEARCH RESOURCES

1) GOVERNMENT AGENCIES
2) PRIVATE AGENCIES
3) JOB HOT LINES
4) CLASSIFIED ADS
5) BULLETIN BOARDS/JOB LISTING BINDERS
6) INTERNET
7) HELP-WANTED SIGNS
8) LIBRARIES
9) JOB FAIRS

Begin with GOVERNMENT AGENCIES and PRIVATE AGENCIES, adding a new resource after each section on pages 94–96 is read by a different student. It will also be helpful to have examples of toll-free numbers and actual classified ads, as well as any other real examples of the other resources (if allowed by prison rules). This way, students will be familiar with what to look for when they are on their own.

Tell the students to look at "General Principles for Responding to Ads for Job Openings" on pages 96–97. Choose different students to read each paragraph aloud. Give the students paper and time to briefly write down the tips for responding to ads for job openings. The following diagram shows what the students should be writing (see page 65 for a transparency master):

TIPS FOR RESPONDING TO JOB OPENINGS

• Respond quickly.
• Be organized.
• No noise or distraction while on the phone.
• Talk cheerfully, with confidence.
• Get job information before you talk about yourself.
• Show enthusiasm.
• Ask for a definitive appointment.

Return to the board/overhead display while reading and discussing "Bulletin Boards and Job Listing Binders" on page 95, "The Internet" on page 96, "Help-Wanted Signs" and "Libraries" on page 98, and "Job Fairs" on page 99.

Ask the following questions:

- *"What items should you bring to a job fair?"* (Answer: Copies of your resume.)

- *"If you see a help-wanted sign in a business that interests you, what should you do?"* (Answer: Go in and apply immediately.)

- *"What information will you find in a library?"* (Answers: Directories of local and national businesses; directories of professional and service organizations in your area.)

- *"If you don't own a computer, where can you find Internet access?"* (Answers: public libraries; friends; relatives; schools.)

- *"What key words would you use if you were searching for jobs on the Internet?"* (Answer: Job and career information.)

- *"What would you ask for if you were looking for a notebook full of job openings and job descriptions?"* (Answer: A job-listing binder.)

Assign pages 99–102 to be read and completed silently.

Read **Challenge** on page 100 aloud to the students. The students can write their ads on that page and then copy them to an index card or sheet of paper to save in their **red folders.** Go over the correct **Checkpoint** answers together as a group.

Checkpoint Answers

1. Employment agencies; job listing binders; the Internet; classified ads; help-wanted signs; libraries; job fairs.

2. Answers will vary.

3. Answers will vary.

4. Answers will vary.

5. Two or three per day is realistic, but a job fair could be a whole-day event.

6. Take your time. Choose the resources that work best for you.

Follow with **Activity #8** if there is time (see page 50).

Activity #1

You've Been Carded!

FORMAT: Individual

TIME: 15–20 minutes

MATERIALS: Five 3 × 5 index cards per student, pens/pencils

1. Write these words in bold print on the board/overhead:

   RESPONSIBILITY, COURAGE, INSPIRATION, MOTIVATION, DEDICATION

2. Review the definition of each word with the class.

3. Give each student five index cards to write the words in capital letters on the blank side of the cards, one word per card.

4. Have the students number the cards in this order: 1. Responsibility, 2. Courage, 3. Inspiration, 4. Motivation, 5. Dedication.

5. On the back of each card, the students will write a phrase and as many responses as they can think of. Here are the phrases:

   Card #1: I will take responsibility for my _____ .

   Card #2: I will have the courage to _____ .

   Card #3: My inspiration will come from _____ .

   Card #4: My motivation to succeed is _____ .

   Card #5: My dedication will show because I will succeed!

6. Have the students place this set of cards in their **red folders.**

Activity #2

Creating a Job Frame-Up

FORMAT: Individual

TIME: 10 minutes

MATERIALS: Frame diagram, pens/pencils

1. Draw the frame diagram shown below on the board/overhead and ask the students to copy it (see page 66 for a transparency master).

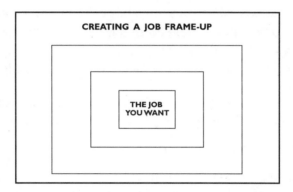

2. Ask the students to write in the innermost box a job that they would like to have. Tell them they must choose realistic careers instead of "superstar" careers.

3. In the middle frame, have them write a skill that they think the job requires.

4. In the outer frame, have them write any way they can think of to get this skill. (Examples: going to school; not giving up; practicing; meeting people.)

5. Tell the students to put the frames in their **red folders**.

Activity #3

The Three "C"s

FORMAT: Individual, then whole class

TIME: 15–20 minutes

MATERIALS: Paper, pens/pencils, situations (see below)

1. Give each student several sheets of paper and a pen or pencil.

2. Say to the class, "We have spent a lot of time talking about solving problems and keeping a positive outlook while thinking about choices and consequences. You have already made some choices and endured the consequences, but how will you make choices when you leave these walls? You will need to make informed decisions based on your knowledge of choices and their possible consequences."

3. Say, "Imagine that you go to your car after grocery shopping. When you open your door, you're shocked to see a huge rattlesnake sitting in the driver's seat. What would you do?"

4. Before the students answer, explain to them that you want to hear what they would do step by step. (Example: First I would close the door, then I would....) Have them write their step-by-step approach on one of the sheets of paper.

5. No matter how simple or complex their answers, explain to the students that they used a decision–making process to figure out what to do. Tell the students that most people use a strategy even if they don't realize it.

6. Teach the students a simple decision-making process by telling them to remember the Three "C"s: Choices, Consequences, Choose.

7. Explain verbally and write the following on the board/overhead:

   Step 1: CHOICES—Think of or write down a list of all the choices available to you. Another word for choices is *alternatives.*

   Step 2: CONSEQUENCES—Think of or write down all the possible consequences, both positive and negative, of each choice. (Think of yourself and the others your choices will affect.)

   Step 3: CHOOSE—Look at all of the consequences and decide which choice will have the most satisfactory results for you and others.

8. Give several possible situations (listed below) and have the students go through the Three "C"s process on their own as you read the situations.

9. Have them write down the Three "C"s on a sheet of paper, followed by the choices, consequences, and "choose" in their situation. Finally, have them make a decision.

10. Share these decisions as a group.

Situations:

#1: You have been feeling bad all morning, and you think it might be slowing you down. Sometimes a clear soft drink helps settle your stomach, but your company doesn't allow soft drinks in the work site. What should you do?

#2: A coworker who is a friend of yours routinely clocks in 10–15 minutes late in the morning and clocks out 10–15 minutes early in the evening. When asked about it by a supervisor, she says she takes only 30 minutes for lunch, because of flexible scheduling options. You know this is untrue. Do you report it?

#3: In the summer months, your company starts a casual dress policy. You really want to wear shorts, but you're not sure if that is acceptable. The company seems very conservative, so you think maybe not. What should you do?

#4: You've never had access to free long-distance phone calls. Even though company policy is to call long distance only for business purposes, you know many coworkers who make personal long-distance calls a few times a week. They say, "Who watches, anyway?" Should you make personal long-distance calls yourself?

#5: In nearly a year of work, you have received highly complimentary evaluations, of which you are very proud. Your coworkers like you, and you're very proud of your success. One afternoon, you're called into your supervisor's office and told that you must pack your things: You've been fired! You are shocked! You ask for documentation and reasons. Your employer says your recent work has been unsatisfactory, and that's it! What should you do?

Activity #4

Times Are A-Changin'

FORMAT: Individual

TIME: 15–20 minutes

MATERIALS: Chart paper, markers

1. Give each student a piece of chart paper and a marker.

2. Ask each student to write the words PRODUCTIVE TIME in the center of the paper.

3. Have each student think of productive ways to spend time and write these ideas in the space around the center words. The drawings might look like this:

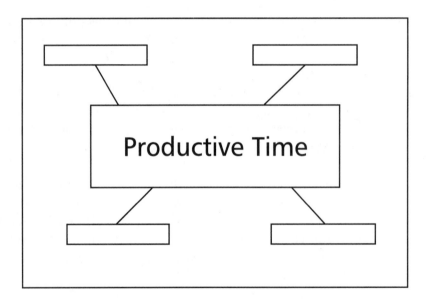

Productive Time

4. As they work on their drawings, ask the students to keep these questions in mind: "How do these activities help you?" and "What are some examples of the ways in which they help you?"

5. Allow time for several students to present their suggested activities and reasoning.

Activity #5

Attitude Adjustment Association

FORMAT: Whole class

TIME: 20 minutes

MATERIALS: Paper, pens/pencils

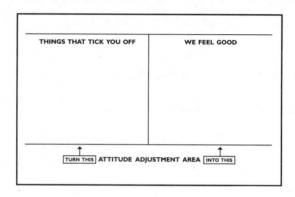

1. Write the following on one-fourth of the board/overhead: THINGS THAT TICK YOU OFF. (See page 67 for a transparency master for the diagram used in this activity.)

2. Hand out paper to each student and instruct them to list anything they can think of that fits under that heading (allow 3–5 minutes).

3. Ask the students to share items from their lists. Write the repeated items on the board under the heading.

4. Write the following heading on another fourth of the board, leaving the first heading and list: WE FEEL GOOD.

5. Have the students list on their papers things that make them feel good.

6. Discuss and write common things under the heading.

7. Use the lower half of the board as the ATTITUDE ADJUSTMENT AREA.

8. Brainstorm with the class ways to make the things that tick them off into things that make them feel good. Write these in the ATTITUDE ADJUSTMENT AREA.

9. Allow time for the students to copy this chart and put it into their **red folders**.

Activity #6

Roadblock Removal

FORMAT: Individual

TIME: 15–20 minutes

MATERIALS: Paper, pens/pencils, chart paper, markers

1. Give each student a sheet of paper and a pen or pencil.

2. Tell the students to write down any roadblock they can think of that might make getting a job difficult for them (allow five minutes).

3. Give each student a sheet of chart paper.

4. Tell them to fold the paper in half. On the right side, write ROADBLOCKS at the top of the column. On the left side, write the word REMOVAL at the top of the column.

5. Allow five minutes. Tell the students to choose at least six items from their first list to write under ROADBLOCKS.

6. Allow five more minutes for the students to brainstorm ways to remove the roadblocks.

7. The students will write these ways under REMOVAL.

8. Suggest that the students write some of these ways on their **red folders.**

Activity #7

Discover Your Resources

FORMAT: Whole class

TIME: 30–45 minutes

MATERIALS: Classified ads from several local newspapers, Internet printouts from several job search Web sites, paper, pens/pencils. (If these are not available, mock-ups may be used for demonstration.)

1. Before the students begin this activity, explain that when they are looking for a job in ads or in books or on the Internet, jobs are grouped by type. For example, **medical jobs** include nurse's aide, medical assistant, and transcriptionist; **professional jobs** include office manager, teacher, and engineer; **technology jobs** include computer programmer and Web designer. The list can go on. Be sure the students understand the concept of grouping jobs by category.

2. Give each student the information sources.

3. Have students compile a list of current job categories and then give five examples of the types of jobs available.

4. Ask them to note which categories list the most available jobs.

5. Have the students organize the categories in order, from the one that requires the most skills to the one that requires the least skills.

6. Begin a discussion in which the students can share their impressions and opinions of their experiences with the job market.

Activity #8

I See, I See

FORMAT: Individual

TIME: 15 minutes

MATERIALS: Paper, pens/pencils, one 3 × 5 index card per student

1. Write the following statement on the board/overhead:

   I can see myself doing _____ because _____ , but I don't ever see myself doing _____ because _____ .

2. Have the students copy and complete the statement on their index cards.

3. This will help focus the students' early job searching.

4. Have the students place these cards in their **red folders.**

Comprehensive Vocabulary Quiz for Book I

THE DOUBLE YOU: THE PERSON YOU ARE AND THE PERSON YOU WANT TO BE

Matching

Directions: *Match the word with the correct definition. Write the letter on the line next to the word.*

1. apprentice ____

2. self-esteem ____

3. expenses ____

4. vocational ____

5. goals ____

6. communication ____

7. resource ____

8. community ____

9. forgiveness ____

10. paranoia ____

a. Things you spend money on.

b. What you work toward achieving.

c. Specific training to fit a job.

d. No more fault or blame.

e. Create an understanding.

f. Overly suspicious and negative.

g. The people around you.

h. The way you feel about yourself.

i. Trained on the job.

j. Any place, person, or thing that provides information and assistance.

Fill in the Blank

Directions: *Choose the word that best fits the sentence.*

1. A _____ is something important to you.

2. An employer may call you to _____ for a job.

3. Many colleges provide _____ to help people match their interests with job openings.

4. You must be _____ and keep trying to reach your goal.

5. A face-to-face argument or disagreement is a _____ .

6. Being suspicious of everyone shows that you have _____ .

7. Anything you have set out to do and completed successfully is an _____ .

8. People who share ideas and work together show _____ .

9. A written statement of your personal values and goals is your _____ .

10. Facing the outside world bravely shows that you are _____ .

career counselors	courageous
mission statement	paranoia
interview	value
persistent	conflict
accomplishment	interview
collaboration	

True or False

Directions: *Write "true" or "false" next to the statement. If the statement is false, change it to make it true.*

1. You can meet potential employers at the **job market.**

   _____

2. Showing a positive, cheerful attitude lets people know you have **enthusiasm.**

   _____

3. Getting everything you want all the time is a form of **compromise.**

   _____

4. Face-to-face personal contact, possibly involving conflict, is a **confrontation.**

   _____

5. Telling half-truths shows **sincerity.**

   _____

6. Doing everything right away is **procrastination.**

   _____

7. No one will be able to tell anything about you by your **attitude.**

   _____

8. A story or song that gives you a positive feeling or idea is **inspiring.**

   _____

9. Accepting the positive and negative results of your actions shows that you have accepted **responsibility.**

   _____

10. Connecting again with family and friends by letter-writing or phone calls means that you are **reestablishing** contacts.

   _____

Answer Key

Matching

1. i
2. h
3. a
4. c
5. b
6. e
7. j
8. g
9. d
10. f

Fill in the Blank

1. value
2. interview
3. career counselor
4. persistent
5. conflict
6. paranoia
7. accomplishment
8. collaboration
9. mission statement
10. courageous

True or False

1. False; You can meet potential employers at a job fair.

2. True

3. False; Giving a little and taking a little is a form of compromise.

4. True

5. False; Telling the truth shows sincerity.

6. False; Waiting until the last minute to do something is procrastination.

7. False; You can tell a lot about someone by noticing his or her attitude.

8. True

9. True

10. True

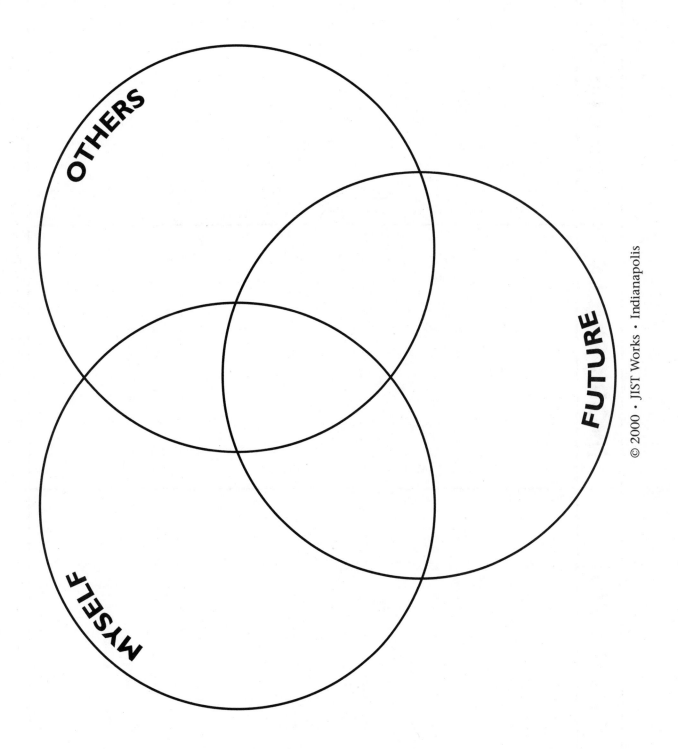

SCHOOL SKILLS	WORK SKILLS	LEISURE SKILLS

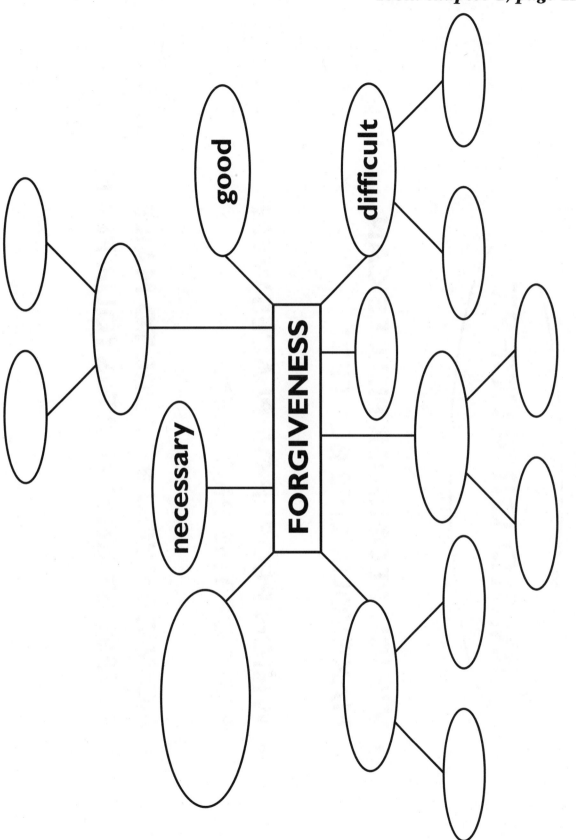

FORGIVENESS

good

difficult

necessary

AVOID OR ACCEPT

- WHICH PEOPLE OR PLACES CAN MAKE YOUR LIFE BETTER?

- WHICH PEOPLE OR PLACES WERE PART OF THE PROBLEM?

- HOW CAN YOU BE SURE TO MAKE A NEW START? WHAT IS YOUR PLAN?

YOUR ATTITUDE		
CHALLENGES FACED	POSITIVE REACTION	NEGATIVE REACTION

© 2000 • JIST Works • Indianapolis

From chapter 3, page 21

TYPES OF COMMUNICATION

SITUATION	VISUAL (BODY)	VERBAL
1) CLERK APPEARS TO STARE AT YOU.		
2) SOMEONE ASKS WHERE YOU'RE FROM.		
3) YOU ARE ASKED IF YOU HAVE TRANSPORTATION.		
4) SOMEONE BUMPS INTO YOU IN A STORE.		
5) A CUSTOMER ASKS IF YOU HAVE SEEN THEIR KEYS.		

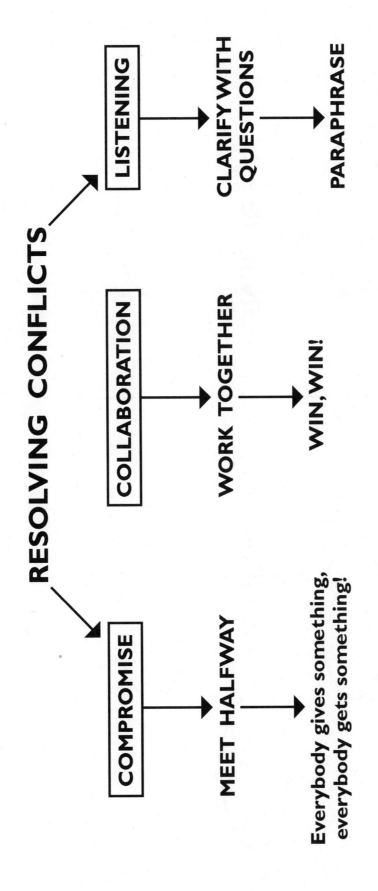

RESOLVING CONFLICTS

COMPROMISE

MEET HALFWAY

Everybody gives something, everybody gets something!

COLLABORATION

WORK TOGETHER

WIN, WIN!

LISTENING

CLARIFY WITH QUESTIONS

PARAPHRASE

ATTACK THE PROBLEM, NOT THE PERSON!

HOW ARE THEY DIFFERENT?

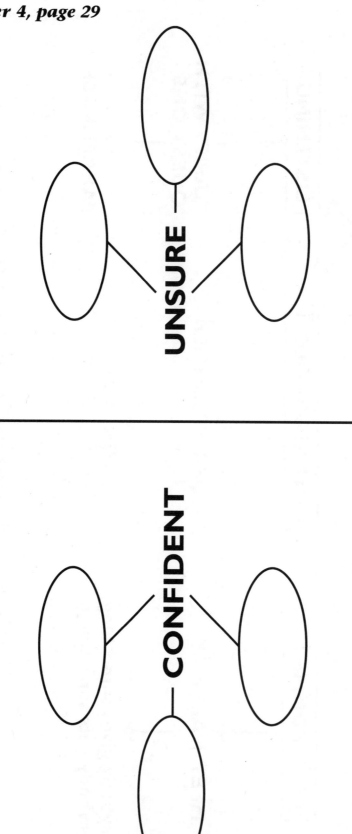

UNSURE

CONFIDENT

EMPLOYMENT AGENCIES

GOVERNMENT

- No fee.

- Also called the "Unemployment Office."

- Employers are able to list job openings there. If you are qualified for a certain job, the office will send you on an interview.

- Only 5 percent of job seekers find jobs through this service.

PRIVATE

- Charge a fee; sometimes paid by the hiring employer.

- You may have to pay a percentage of your first year's wages if you're hired through an agency.

- Although agencies place want ads for openings they know about, jobs are often gone very quickly.

- 5 percent of job seekers find work this way.

- How they work: The agency calls employers to find out about job openings, then matches the openings with qualified registered people.

From chapter 5, page 40

JOB SEARCH RESOURCES

1) GOVERNMENT AGENCIES

2) PRIVATE AGENCIES

3) JOB HOT LINES

4) CLASSIFIED ADS

5) BULLETIN BOARDS/JOB LISTING BINDERS

6) INTERNET

7) HELP-WANTED SIGNS

8) LIBRARIES

9) JOB FAIRS

TIPS FOR RESPONDING TO JOB OPENINGS

- **Respond quickly.**

- **Be organized.**

- **No noise or distraction while on the phone.**

- **Talk cheerfully, with confidence.**

- **Get job information before you talk about yourself.**

- **Show enthusiasm.**

- **Ask for a definitive appointment.**

From activity #2, page 43

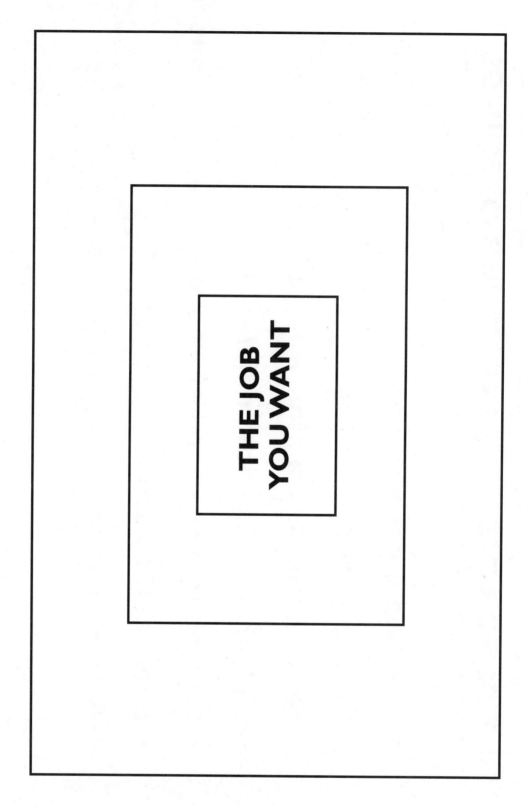

CREATING A JOB FRAME-UP

THE JOB
YOU WANT

From activity #5, page 47

WE FEEL GOOD

THINGS THAT TICK YOU OFF

ATTITUDE ADJUSTMENT AREA

INTO THIS

TURN THIS

PART II

Instructor's Resources for

BEING "JOB-READY":
IDENTIFY YOUR SKILLS, STRENGTHS, AND CAREER GOALS

BEING "JOB-READY":
IDENTIFY YOUR SKILLS, STRENGTHS, AND CAREER GOALS

■ IDENTIFY YOUR STRENGTHS AND MOST IMPORTANT SKILLS.

■ DOCUMENT YOUR WORK EXPERIENCE, INTERESTS, AND LIFE EXPERIENCES TO HELP YOU IDENTIFY CAREER OPTIONS.

■ DEVELOP SHORT- AND LONG-TERM TRAINING, EDUCATION, AND CAREER GOALS.

Ronald C. Mendlin
and Marc Polonsky
with J. Michael Farr

THE PUTTING THE BARS BEHIND YOU SERIES

jist Publishing

JIST's Putting the Bars Behind You Series Instructor's Resource Manual

Workbook Table of Contents

Being "Job-Ready": Identify Your Skills, Strengths, and Career Goals

CHAPTER TWO: Identify Your Experience

CHAPTER THREE: Identify Your Skills

CHAPTER FOUR: Put It All into Action

© JIST Works, Indianapolis, IN

BEING "JOB-READY":
IDENTIFY YOUR SKILLS, STRENGTHS, AND CAREER GOALS

Ronald C. Mendlin
and Marc Polonsky
with J. Michael Farr

Your Foundation

CHAPTER OBJECTIVES

1. To look at your work and life experience and point out the skills you've gained.

2. To learn the difference between a strength and a skill.

3. To identify your strengths.

4. To identify your preferred work environments.

Working Vocabulary

● **Experience.** Anything you have lived through is an *experience*. *Experience* can also mean previous jobs you have had.

● **Skill.** Anything you have learned and can do well is a *skill*.

● **Strength.** A natural ability or talent is a *strength*.

● **Priorities.** Things that are more important to do than others are *priorities*.

Presentation Suggestions

Begin by introducing the book and explaining to the students that the focus of this text is different than the first book. This book focuses on their skills and strengths, which will bring them closer to getting a steady, secure job. You can use the board/overhead to display their ideas about the benefits of holding a job and how to know when they are job-ready. The following diagram shows how to set this up (see page 101 for a transparency master):

SKILLS + STRENGTHS = JOB GOAL	
BENEFITS OF A JOB	BE JOB-READY BY...

Follow with **Activity #1** (see page 92). This activity is an introduction to get the students to think about job titles and skills that go with them. This activity will help clarify the focus of the entire workbook: identifying job skills.

Next, read aloud all the **Working Vocabulary** words and definitions for this chapter. Use chart paper or the board/overhead to create a display of vocabulary words from all the chapters. Add the new words and definitions for each chapter to this display as you begin each chapter.

After presenting the vocabulary words, discuss the **Chapter Objectives.** Ask the students to check off the objectives when they feel each one has been met.

Invite a student to read aloud "Make the Most of Your Experience" on page 4. Ask the following question:

● *"Have you ever thought about the fact that these experiences can give you useful skills?"* (Accept any appropriate responses.)

Complete **Think About It** on pages 5–6. Follow with **Activity #2** (see page 93).

Ask a student to read aloud "Strengths and Skills: What's the Difference?" on page 7. Use the board/overhead to discuss how strengths and skills are similar to one another, and how they are different from one another. The following diagram shows how to set this up (see page 102 for a transparency master):

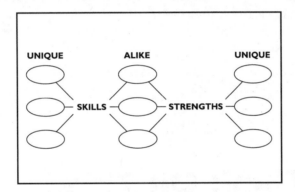

Assign "Define Your Strengths" to be read silently. Have the students complete pages 8–9.

Give each student a **green folder.** Students will use this just like they did the **red folder** in the first workbook in this series. It will be used to collect and organize useful information. Ask the students to write their names in bold letters at the top of the front of the folder.

Then give each student two index cards. Have the students write STRENGTHS on one and SKILLS on the other. Give them time to write their three best strengths on the back of the first card. Next, have them look at the three strengths and think of three skills that can be developed from those strengths. Have the students put these cards in their **green folders.**

Read aloud and discuss "Work Priorities: What's Important to You?" on page 10. Remind the students of the definition of *priority.* Say, "Let's name some priorities in your lives." Write these on the board/overhead. (If students will not share, you can write down some priorities yourself.) Discuss which of these priorities are most important, less important, and not very important. You can have students do this out loud or in a game-show format, where you state the priority and the students call out "very," "less," or "not." You can have fun with this if your students can handle the action.

Assign pages 10–11 to be completed individually. When the students have finished pages 10–11, have them write four or five "1"s from the list on the front of their **green folders** under the heading PRIORITIES.

Have the students complete the **Checkpoint** on page 12. When they are done, discuss the answers with the class.

Checkpoint Answers

1. A strength is a natural ability or talent; a skill is something you have learned to do.

2. Answers will vary.

3. Answers will vary.

4. Answers will vary.

Think On This...

● What work or school experience have you had?

● Did you ever enjoy any of it?

● Do you have a favorite hobby, even if it's something that you haven't been able to do since you've been in prison?

● Can you think of any jobs that might be almost like your hobby?

● What are they?

● If someone asked you to do your hobby for money, would you think about it?

Chapter Two

Identify Your Experience

CHAPTER OBJECTIVES

1. To remember and write down all of your work experience.

2. To remember and write down all of your school and training history.

3. To think about and write down all hobbies and enjoyable activities.

4. To remember all places and things that have provided skills.

Working Vocabulary

- **Responsibility.** Taking *responsibility* means accepting the good and bad outcomes of your actions without blaming someone else.

- **Hobby.** A *hobby* is something enjoyable or fun that you do to fill your free time.

- **Vocational.** Training that is *vocational* relates specifically to a particular job.

- **Accomplishment.** Anything that you have completed successfully is an *accomplishment*.

Presentation Suggestions

Begin by introducing the **Chapter Objectives**. Point out that this chapter involves a lot of writing. You will need to be available to help students who do not write well.

Use the following diagram to show students what they will be writing about and in what order (see page 103 for a transparency master):

WRITING ABOUT:

- **Our work experience**
- **Our school and training**
- **Our hobbies**

Ask the following question:

- *"What things do you think you will be writing about?"* (Answer: work experience, school and training, and hobbies.)

Then introduce the **Working Vocabulary,** adding it to the list from chapter 1.

Ask the students to complete the **School Worksheet** on page 14 and the **Training Worksheet** on page 15. Have the students pull out these pages and place them in their **green folders.**

Ask a student to read aloud "Work Experience" on page 16. Then have the students complete pages 16–17 on their own.

Continue to read aloud "Activities and Hobbies: What Do You Like to Do?" on page 18. Then give the students time to complete the individual work on page 18 (about five minutes).

Have a student volunteer read aloud "What Else?" on page 19, and allow five minutes for the students to complete the written work. Follow with **Activity #3** if you want (see page 94).

Tell the students to complete **Checkpoint** on page 20. When they are done, talk about the possible answers and ask if anyone wants to share what they wrote.

Quick Quiz

Name: _____

Directions: *Complete the crossword puzzle. The answers are vocabulary words from chapters 1 and 2.*

Across

1. Specific training

4. Most important

5. Jobs you have had

6. Army, Navy, Air Force, Marines, Coast Guard

8. What you do for fun

9. Formal education after high school

Down

2. What you have achieved

3. A natural talent

7. A learned talent

Quick Quiz Answer Key

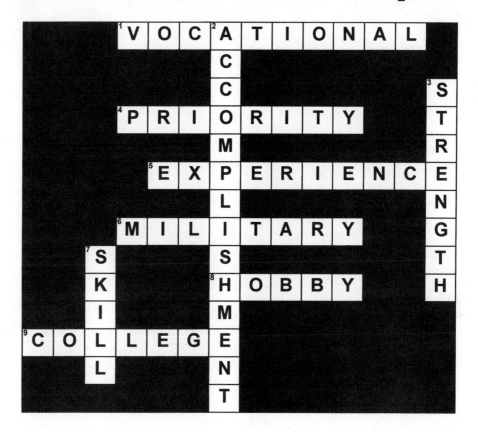

Crossword answers:
1. VOCATIONAL
2. ACCOMPLISHMENT
3. STRENGTH
4. PRIORITY
5. EXPERIENCE
6. MILITARY
7. SKILL
8. HOBBY
9. COLLEGE

Think On This...

● Think about all your skills.

● Now, think about just one of them.

● For you to be good at the one big skill, what small things do you need to be skilled at? For example, if your skill is auto mechanics, you are also good at organizing, solving problems, mathematics, and working with tools.

Chapter Three

Identify Your Skills

CHAPTER OBJECTIVES

1. To learn to break your major skills into several smaller skills.

2. To take a complete inventory of your skills, both major and smaller.

3. To determine what skills you'd like to use most in the future and which skills you'd like to gain or improve.

Working Vocabulary

- **Personality skill (adaptive skill).** An *adaptive skill* is part of your personality that you use every day to survive and get along.

- **Transferable skill (general job-related skill).** A *transferable skill* is anything you do well that you could learn on one job and take with you to use on another job.

- **Specific job-related skill.** A *specific job-related skill* is the ability to do anything that is particular to a specific job.

- **Inventory.** An *inventory* is a detailed listing of contents or experiences.

- **Leisure.** Free time to do something fun is *leisure* time.

Presentation Suggestions

Begin the chapter by rereading aloud **Think On This...** from the end of chapter 1. Then read the **Chapter Objectives** for chapter 2 out loud. Ask the students to tell you what is similar between both of them.

Then ask them to listen to **Think On This...** from chapter 2. Ask the students to guess the objectives for chapter 3. Write these guesses on the board/overhead. Then read aloud the actual chapter 3 objectives, giving students time to discuss how closely their guesses match the actual objectives.

Present the **Working Vocabulary**, adding the chapter 3 words to those from chapters 1 and 2.

Ask a student to read aloud "Break Down Your Skills" on page 22. Ask students to help you break down a familiar skill such as baking a pizza. Use the following diagram to create a board/overhead display for the skills breakdown by listing the skills you use when baking a pizza (see page 104 for a transparency master):

> **SKILL: BAKE A PIZZA**
>
> **BREAKDOWN →**
> 1)
> 2)
> 3)
> 4)
> 5)
> 6)

Have the students complete **Think About It** on page 23 individually. If time allows and the students are willing, ask volunteers to share one of the major skills they wrote down and how they broke it down into smaller skills.

Invite a student to read "Different Types of Skills" on page 24. Say, "In chapter 2 you learned about school skills, work skills, and hobby skills. Those categories refer to the places those skills are used. Now we're using the terms *adaptive, transferable,* and *job-related.* These categories refer to the actual skills." Review the definitions of each type of skill.

Use the following diagram to organize the following activity as well as to remind the students how the skill types are different (see page 105 for a transparency master):

SKILLS		
JOB-RELATED: SKILLS YOU LEARN ON THE JOB	TRANSFERABLE: CAN APPLY THESE SKILLS TO MANY DIFFERENT JOBS	ADAPTIVE: PERSONALITY AND PEOPLE SKILLS

Then say, "I will read a list of skills that I have written on index cards. As I read each skill, I will ask one of you to take the card and stick it on the board in the correct column." (If you are using an overhead, make a transparency of the skills. Then cut the skills into individual pieces and have the students put these in the correct columns on the overhead.) Put the following skills on the index cards (the answers are in parentheses):

sensitivity (A)	following instructions (T)
money management (T)	building an engine (J)
problem-solving (T)	ability to stay calm (A)
tuning a piano (J)	handling several things at once (T)
enthusiasm (A)	good attendance (A)
communication (T)	good writing skills (T)
being on time (A)	using your hands (T)
ability to plan ahead (T)	patience (A)
teamwork (T)	using the Internet (T)

After this exercise, be sure each skill is in the correct column. Answer any questions the students may have.

Ask a student to read aloud "Your Personality Skills" on page 24. Follow with **Activity #4** (see page 95).

Have a student read aloud "Identify Your Personality Skills and General Skills" on page 25. Then read the instructions for the **Personality Skills Worksheet** to the students and make sure they understand them. Complete the **Personality Skills Worksheet** on pages 26–28. Allow time for the students to write their top three personality skills on the front of their **green folders** under the heading MY TOP PERSONALITY SKILLS.

Ask a student to read aloud "Your General Job Skills" on page 29. Have the students complete the **General Job Skills Worksheet** on pages 30–36. Allow at least 20 minutes, because there is a lot of material to get through. Ask the students to write the heading MY TOP GENERAL JOB SKILLS on their **green folders,** and then their top job skills.

Complete the **Checkpoint** on pages 37–38. Discuss the correct answers with the class.

Checkpoint Answers

1. Adaptive skills that are used daily to deal with people.

2. Transferable skills that can be used in many job situations.

3. Being able to tell an employer your skills will make the employer more willing to hire you.

Read aloud the instructions for **Think About It** on page 38. Tell the students to look at pages 39–41. Explain that they will be completing these pages based on the "top" skills they wrote down in the preceding exercises. Tell the class that they will be tearing these pages out and placing them in their **green folders** when they are done.

Ask a student to read aloud "Take Inventory of Your Skills" on page 42.

Read the **Skills Inventory Worksheet** directions to the class. Then ask a student to reread the directions. Answer any questions the students may have about this section. Then give the students about 30 minutes to complete pages 43–51. Follow with **Activity #5** (see page 96).

Complete the **Checkpoint** on page 52 in small groups and discuss the answers—they will vary. (This is the first time we have suggested breaking the class into small groups. If you don't think your class is ready for this, discuss the responses as a class.)

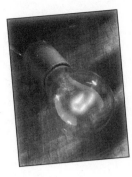

Think On This...

- Have you thought of a realistic career direction you would like to go in?

- Where would you begin looking for information about that career?

- What if you find out that getting that job means you have to go back to school? Are you still interested?

- What if reaching that goal means working at a fast food restaurant to pay for school and not doing much socializing? Are you still interested? Think about it. It could happen!

Chapter Four

Put It All into Action

CHAPTER OBJECTIVES

1. To think about the kind of career that is most interesting to you.

2. To learn where to look for career information.

3. To realize that sometimes it's worth passing up small pleasures to achieve long-term goals.

4. To improve your skills through training and education.

5. To start setting concrete job and career–related goals for yourself.

Working Vocabulary

● **Career.** A job in a field you've chosen that lasts for several years is a *career*. Your career can also include jobs you had in other places, if the jobs are similar to one another.

● **Search engine.** Places on the Internet where people begin their online searching are called *search engines*. Some examples of *search engines* are Yahoo! and Infoseek.

Presentation Suggestions

Begin by restating **Think On This...** from the end of chapter 3. Ask the students to guess what the **Chapter Objectives** are for chapter 4. Write their suggestions on the board/overhead. Then read the actual objectives and compare them to the guesses.

Add the new **Working Vocabulary** words to the lists from the other chapters and discuss. Explain that the focus of this chapter is on using job search materials in a way that works for you.

Ask a student to read aloud "The Right Job for You" on page 54. Ask the following questions:

● *"Why are so many people unhappy with their jobs?"* (Answer: They let other people tell them what jobs they should do.)

● *"What is it called when you explore many different careers and think about which jobs suit you best?"* (Answer: Career planning.)

Have another student read "Start to Think About Careers" on pages 54–55. Ask the following question:

● *"If you don't have the exact skills for a job, but a company is willing to hire you, what might that company offer to do?"* (Answer: Pay for your training to do the job.)

Have a student read the first two paragraphs of "Jobs That Match Your Skills" on pages 55–56. Have the students read the categories silently. Discuss these categories by playing a game. The diagram on the next page shows the game board display (see page 106 for a transparency master).

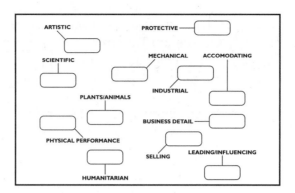

Divide the class into two teams. Write each of the following job titles on a 3 × 5 card (write the titles before the class starts, to save time in class):

gym teacher	car salesman	veterinary technician
computer technician	paralegal	nurse
social worker	construction worker	photographer
limo driver	carpenter	

Call two students, one from each team, up to the front of the room. Give these students several clues about the job title you are holding. Continue to give clues one at a time until one of the students guesses the correct job title. Then give the card to that student and have him place it in the correct category. If he does both parts correctly, his team gets 2 points. If he misses the category match, only 1 point is given. Continue to call different students to the front of the room until you've gone through all the cards. The team with the most points wins.

Choose several students to take turns reading aloud "Gather Information" and "Keep an Open Mind" on pages 56–58. Then have the students list five to ten occupations that interest them in **Think About It** on page 58.

Pages 59–68 are **Job Information Worksheets**. Read aloud the two paragraphs at the bottom of page 58. Have the students look at the information required on the sheets and ask any questions about the information. Then have the students pull these pages out and put them in their **green folders** so that they can use the worksheets after they are released from prison.

Invite a student to read aloud "Training Now Will Pay Off Later" on page 69. Ask the following question:

- *"Why is training helpful in the long run?"* (Answers: More job security; more job choices; better pay.)

Have another student read "Formal Schooling" on page 70. Have other students take turns reading "The Military," "On-the-Job Training," and "Apprenticeships" on page 71. Use the following diagram to organize the information from pages 70–71 on the board/overhead in an easy-to-read table (see page 107 for a transparency master):

NORMAL SCHOOLING	TRAINING OPTIONS		
	MILITARY	ON-THE-JOB	APPRENTICESHIPS

Fill in details of each training type as they are read aloud. Then give each student a sheet of paper and tell them to copy the completed chart onto it. Have the students put the chart in their **green folders**.

Read "Improve Your General Skills" on page 72 aloud to the class. Have the students complete **Think About It** on page 72.

Ask for a student volunteer to read aloud "Resources for Learning General Skills" at the bottom of page 72. Ask the following question:

- *"What are the good things about community training programs?"* (Answers: Low cost; wide range of programs; convenient times; in the area.)

Have a student read "Career Research Pointers" on page 73 to the class. Ask the following question:

- *"Describe several ways to get career pointers."* (Answers: Talk to people in the field; arrange informal talks [informational interviews] with people who work in the fields in which you are interested.)

Read aloud "Short-Term and Long-Term Goals" at the bottom of page 73, including the questions. Then have the students complete page 74 on their own. Be available to help students who need individual help.

Ask a student to read aloud "Keep Your Goals Realistic and Manageable" on pages 74–75. Complete the **Worksheets** on pages 75–76 together as a group.

Ask another student to read aloud "Action Plans" on page 77. Be sure to carefully go over the example on page 77. If needed, you can copy it onto a transparency sheet to use as an overhead. Then allow 20–25 minutes for students to write down action and back-up plans on pages 78–83. Have the students pull out these pages and put them in their **green folders.**

Read aloud "Daily Action Plans" on page 84. Then have the students pull out the **Daily Planning Worksheet** on pages 84–85 for later use and put it in their **green folders.**

Have a student read aloud "Final Words About Goals" on page 86.

Have the students complete **Checkpoint** on pages 87–89. Discuss the answers with the students.

After completing and discussing **Checkpoint,** follow with **Activity #6.** It will give the students a chance to get their hands on the reference books discussed in chapter 4.

Checkpoint Answers

1. Handbooks, talking to people, the Internet.

2. How do you enter the field? Do you need much training? Is there a good future? How much money can you make? Does it offer job security? What skills are needed?

3. So that you can achieve bigger goals later.

4. School, military, on-the-job training.

5. Who can help me? What goals must I reach first? What obstacles might come between my goals and me? How will I get past these obstacles?

6. Break goals into steps.

7. What you will do each day to reach your goals.

Activity #1

Job Associations

FORMAT: Individual, then group

TIME: 25–30 minutes

MATERIALS: Chart paper, markers, pens/pencils, index cards—each with a job title written on it

1. Give each student one card. Give them a short time to write their ideas of what the job is about on the back of the card.

2. Call on students to read aloud what they have written. List the jobs on the board/overhead as they are read. Continue this until all students have read their cards.

3. Return students' attention to the card in front of them and ask them to write down what they believe are three skills needed to perform the job and at least one skill that is used only for that job.

4. Break the class into groups of four or five.

5. Give the groups about 10 minutes to discuss the jobs and compare the skills they have written down, looking for things that are the same.

6. Give each group a piece of chart paper and a marker. Ask each group to write down the skills it came up with in order of the most common (the one the most people wrote down) to the least common.

7. Come back together as a class and discuss the repeated skills. List these on a piece of chart paper to be displayed in the room for the rest of the course.

Activity #2

TWL (Talk, Write, Listen)

FORMAT: Paired

TIME: 20–25 minutes

MATERIALS: Pens/pencils, paper, timer

1. Tell the students to look at the experiences they listed on pages 5 and 6.

2. Tell the students to think of one of the experiences in detail—one that they can recall well enough to make a story out of it.

3. Explain that each student will be given a partner for this activity.

4. Assign partners, choosing one student to be partner A and the other to be partner B.

5. Ask all partner Bs to raise their hands.

6. Explain that partner B will tell his experience story first (give him three minutes) while partner A listens. Then tell partner A to write anything he remembers from his partner's story, as well as any skills he thinks were used in the experience (allow three minutes).

7. Reverse the exercise so that partner A talks and partner B writes.

8. Allow time for the class to share their answers by asking, "Did anyone find that his partner identified a skill he didn't know he had?"

Activity #3

All of the Above

FORMAT: Small group

TIME: 10–20 minutes

MATERIALS: Chart paper, markers, listing of job titles from the end of the workbook

1. Assign the students to groups of three or four.

2. Give each group a piece of chart paper and a copy of the Appendix from the back of the workbook. Tell the students to fold the paper into three columns.

3. Ask the groups to label the three columns as follows: WORK SKILLS, SCHOOL SKILLS, HOBBY SKILLS.

4. Have the group choose any job title they would like from the list of jobs. (Tell them that at least one person in the group should know a little about the chosen job title.)

5. Have the students list what they feel are the needed skills in each column based on the job they've chosen.

6. Ask them to read their skill chart to the class.

Activity #4

Trait Tree

FORMAT: Individual

TIME: 15–20 minutes

MATERIALS: White paper, pens/pencils, one copy of the following diagram for each student

1. Show the following diagram in an enlarged size on the board/overhead (see page 108 for a transparency master).

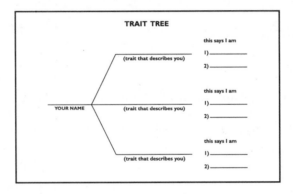

2. Discuss the word *trait* as it relates to people's personalities. (It is a descriptive word used to tell about a part of someone's personality.)

3. Give each student a copy of the preceding diagram.

4. Fill in the demo diagram on the board/overhead, using your own traits as an example.

5. Have the students fill in their personal trait trees.

6. Ask the students to volunteer to share their trait trees.

Activity #5

Obstacles Abound

FORMAT: Individual, then group

TIME: 20–25 minutes

MATERIALS: Paper, pens/pencils, 4 × 8 index cards (two per student)

1. Show the following headings on the board/overhead:

   SKILLS I HAVE

   SKILLS I WANT TO IMPROVE

   WAYS TO IMPROVE

2. Give each student a 4 × 8 card on which they will write the headings.

3. Give the students time to make a chart by listing their responses under each heading; set the cards aside.

4. Explain to the class that they should think back on the skills they have. They should try to remember when they were learning those skills. Tell them that the things that made a skill more difficult to learn or that got in the way of learning are *obstacles*.

5. Ask, "What were some of the obstacles to learning some of the skills you now have?" Take all comments and write several on the board/overhead.

6. Break the class into small groups.

7. The groups should discuss more obstacles to learning skills and some positive ways to deal with them. Giving up is never an option!

8. Come back as a class after about three minutes. On the board/overhead, write a list of obstacles and ways to deal with them.

9. Give each student a second 4 × 6 card on which to write OBSTACLES on one side and WAYS TO DEAL WITH on the other.

10. Have the students place both 4 × 6 cards in their **green folders**.

Activity #6

Book Pass

FORMAT: Small group

TIME: 20–25 minutes

MATERIALS: Reference books discussed in chapter 4, timer, paper, pens/pencils

1. Give each group one of the books listed as a reference in chapter 4.

2. Allow the group members to scan the book and write down several brief pieces of information, as well as what they think about the book overall. Allow three to five minutes per book (set the timer).

3. Repeat the process, passing each book from group to group when the timer goes off.

4. When each group has looked at each book, allow students to talk about the titles they examined.

Comprehensive Vocabulary Quiz for Book 2

BEING "JOB-READY": IDENTIFY YOUR SKILLS, STRENGTHS, AND CAREER GOALS

Name: _____

Directions: *Tell whether the statement is true or false. If the statement is false, change it to make it true. Then find the **bold-faced** words in the puzzle.*

1. A **search engine** is what keeps your car running.

   True _____   False _____

2. Anything you have tried and failed at is an **accomplishment.**

   True _____   False _____

3. A **career** is a job you have for a short time.

   True _____   False _____

4. **Job-related** training is very general and can be found anywhere.

   True _____   False _____

5. Your **priority** is what you do last of all.

   True _____   False _____

6. Being sensitive to others' feelings uses your **adaptive** skills.

   True _____   False _____

7. Painting to relax is an example of a **hobby.**

   True _____   False _____

8. A detailed list of the contents of anything is an **inventory.**

   True _____   False _____

9. An employer does not look at your **experience** when considering you for a job.

10. **Leisure** time is time that is scheduled exactly.

    True _____   False _____

11. You should accept **responsibility** for your actions.

    True _____   False _____

12. A **strength** is something you are not good at doing.

    True _____   False _____

13. A learned ability is a **skill.**

    True _____   False _____

14. **Transferable** skills can be used at many different types of jobs.

    True _____   False _____

15. Only singers need **vocational** training.

    True _____   False _____

T	N	E	M	H	S	I	L	P	M	O	C	C	A	Y
P	P	S	T	R	E	N	G	T	H	Z	C	U	T	D
D	A	E	X	P	E	R	I	E	N	C	E	I	D	D
J	H	A	A	X	M	G	S	K	I	L	L	C	R	E
C	K	R	D	H	X	R	D	X	P	I	V	Z	E	T
U	K	C	A	K	K	L	E	Y	B	B	O	H	Y	A
D	N	H	P	U	Z	V	Y	I	Y	I	C	Y	J	L
Z	G	E	T	R	A	N	S	F	E	R	A	B	L	E
I	X	N	I	N	N	Q	I	U	G	T	M	O	R	
C	Z	G	V	F	O	Y	T	I	R	O	I	R	P	B
Q	F	I	E	P	I	N	V	E	N	T	O	R	Y	O
L	S	N	S	U	E	V	P	F	Z	U	N	S	D	J
I	L	E	I	S	U	R	E	H	O	G	A	D	Q	C
F	R	E	E	R	A	C	X	C	U	O	L	K	M	T

Answer Key

1. False. A **search engine** is used to find information on the Internet.

2. False. An **accomplishment** is anything you have done well.

3. False. A **career** is the series of jobs you have had in your lifetime.

4. False. **Job-related** training is specific to one particular job.

5. False. Your **priority** is what you do first.

6. True.

7. True.

8. True.

9. False. An employer looks at your **experience** when considering you for a job.

10. False. **Leisure** time is unscheduled time that you spend doing whatever you want to do.

11. True.

12. False. A **strength** is something you are naturally good at doing.

13. True.

14. True.

15. False. **Vocational** training is for any skill or trade that you might want to pursue as a career.

T	N	E	M	H	S	I	L	P	M	O	C	C	A	Y
P	P	S	T	R	E	N	G	T	H	Z	C	U	T	D
D	A	E	X	P	E	R	I	E	N	C	E	I	D	D
J	H	A	A	X	M	G	S	K	I	L	L	C	R	E
C	K	R	D	H	X	R	D	X	P	I	V	Z	E	T
U	K	C	A	K	K	L	E	Y	B	B	O	H	Y	A
D	N	H	P	U	Z	V	Y	I	Y	I	C	Y	J	L
Z	G	E	T	R	A	N	S	F	E	R	A	B	L	E
I	X	N	I	I	N	N	Q	I	U	G	T	M	O	R
C	Z	G	V	F	O	Y	T	I	R	O	I	R	P	B
Q	F	I	E	P	I	N	V	E	N	T	O	R	Y	O
L	S	N	S	U	E	V	P	F	Z	U	N	S	D	J
I	L	E	I	S	U	R	E	H	O	G	A	D	Q	C
F	R	E	E	R	A	C	X	C	U	O	L	K	M	T

SKILLS + STRENGTHS = JOB GOAL

BE JOB-READY BY...

BENEFITS OF A JOB

From chapter 1, page 73

UNIQUE

STRENGTHS

ALIKE

SKILLS

UNIQUE

WRITING ABOUT:

- **Our work experience**
- **Our school and training**
- **Our hobbies**

From chapter 3, page 82

SKILL: BAKE A PIZZA

BREAKDOWN→

1)

2)

3)

4)

5)

6)

SKILLS

JOB-RELATED: SKILLS YOU LEARN ON THE JOB	TRANSFERABLE: CAN APPLY THESE SKILLS TO MANY DIFFERENT JOBS	ADAPTIVE: PERSONALITY AND PEOPLE SKILLS

From chapter 4, page 89

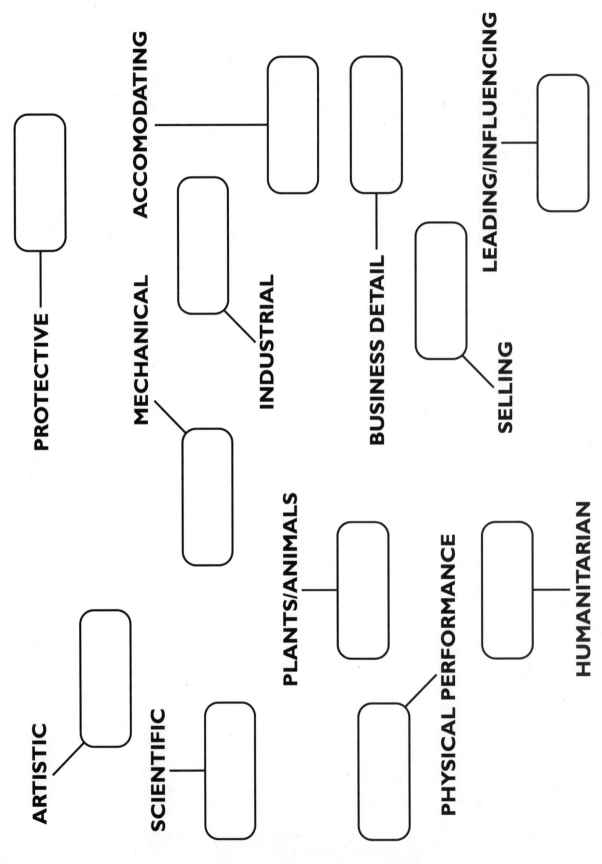

PROTECTIVE

ACCOMODATING

MECHANICAL

INDUSTRIAL

BUSINESS DETAIL

LEADING/INFLUENCING

SELLING

ARTISTIC

SCIENTIFIC

PLANTS/ANIMALS

PHYSICAL PERFORMANCE

HUMANITARIAN

TRAINING OPTIONS

NORMAL SCHOOLING	MILITARY	ON-THE-JOB	APPRENTICESHIPS

© 2000 • JIST Works • Indianapolis

From activity #4, page 95

TRAIT TREE

YOUR NAME

(trait that describes you)

this says I am

1) _____

2) _____

(trait that describes you)

this says I am

1) _____

2) _____

(trait that describes you)

this says I am

1) _____

2) _____

PART III

Instructor's Resources for

JOB SEARCH TOOLS:

RESUMES, APPLICATIONS, AND COVER LETTERS

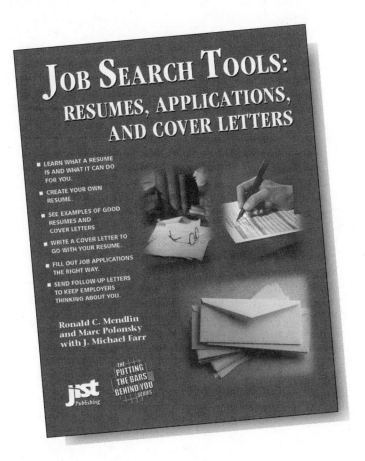

Workbook Table of Contents

Job Search Tools: Resumes, Applications, and Cover Letters

CHAPTER ONE: Resumes

CHAPTER TWO: Job Applications

CHAPTER THREE: Cover Letters and Follow-Up Letters

Resumes

CHAPTER OBJECTIVES

1. To learn what a resume is and why it is important.

2. To learn what should go on a resume.

3. To see what good resumes look like.

4. To make a written inventory of skills, work experience, and accomplishments that can go on a resume.

5. To learn why different jobs may require different resumes.

Working Vocabulary

- **Resume.** A complete written listing of a person's work experience, education, and skills that are related to a particular job is a *resume*.

- **Qualification.** A skill or achievement level that is required in order to be considered for a job opening is a *qualification*.

- **Reference.** A *reference* is a person an employer may contact to find out more about someone applying for a job.

- **Tailoring.** Designing anything to fit a specific purpose is *tailoring*.

- **Slant.** Emphasizing different skills when applying for different jobs is to *slant* your resume.

- **Application.** An *application* is a form that a company asks you to fill out to summarize your experiences and education in a standard way.

Presentation Suggestions

Read the **Chapter Objectives** for chapter 1. Ask the students to identify the overall theme of the chapter as they see it. They should come up with the word *resumes*. If not, guide them to the correct response by asking them to identify the word that appears most often in the **Chapter Objectives.**

Next, present the **Working Vocabulary** words. You should keep these on a board that is reserved for vocabulary words, or on chart paper, or on a transparency sheet. This way, you can add to the list with each chapter and keep it on display during lessons and assignments. Encourage the students to use vocabulary words in their questions and written responses.

Ask a student to read aloud "What Is a Resume, and Do You Need One?" on page 4. Continue reading "How Long Should Your Resume Be?" Ask the following questions:

- *"What is a resume?"* (Answer: A written description of yourself, your job qualifications, and your work experience.)

- *"How long should your resume be?"* (Answer: Just one page.)

Call on another student to read aloud "What Goes on a Resume?" on pages 4 and 5. As the student reads each item aloud, write it on the board/overhead so that you can go back and talk about them later. The diagram on the next page shows how this will look (see page 135 for a transparency master).

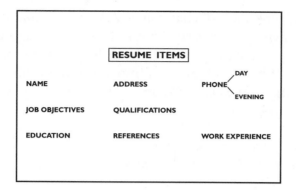

Keep this chart up as you move on to the next section. This way, you can add text to make items clearer if needed.

Call on a volunteer to read aloud "What Is a Job Objective? Why Is It Important?" on page 5. Ask the following question:

● *"Tell me in your own words what a job objective is and why you need to have one."* (Answer: A statement of what type of work you are looking for; it shows the employer that you are focused and know what kind of work you want to do.)

Ask the students to complete the **Job Objective Worksheet** at the bottom of page 5. Explain that these statements must be brief and to the point. Write several good responses on the board/overhead as examples.

At this point, give each student a **blue folder.** Have the class copy their job objectives onto the front of the folder under the heading "_____'s Job Objectives." The students will use this folder to collect, compile, and organize information that will help them in the future.

Invite a student to read aloud the sections about functional resumes (paragraphs 2 and 4) in "The Different Kinds of Resumes" on pages 6 and 7. Begin to create a board/ overhead display that contrasts each resume type. The following diagram shows how this will look (see page 136 for a transparency master):

TYPES OF RESUMES		
FUNCTIONAL	COMBINATION	CHRONOLOGICAL

Give the students a blank sheet of chart paper. Ask them to fold the paper into three even columns. Tell them to label each column the same as the columns on the board/overhead. Explain that while the board/overhead display is created, they will copy the information that they find most important into the columns on their own piece of paper. They can reword or use abbreviations as they wish; however, they will want to be able to read what they've written.

Ask another student to read aloud pages 7 and 8, the sections about chronological resumes (paragraphs 3 and 5). Follow the same pattern as before.

When the students have finished adding to their personal charts for functional and chronological resumes, tell them to look at the sample resumes on pages 8 and 9. If you're using an overhead projector, copy these examples onto transparency sheets and point out each section as you review it. Ask the following questions:

- *"Which sections are in the same order on both resumes?"* (Answer: Name, address, phone number, job objective, and highlights of qualifications.)

- *"How are the* Relevant Skills and Experience *sections different?"* (Answer: A functional resume spells out each individual skill in detail but does not include specific dates; a chronological resume includes the skills with the past work experience and dates.)

- *"Which resume do you think is easier to read and understand, and why?"* (Answer: Answers will vary.)

Move on to page 10 and have a student read aloud "The Best Kind of Resume: The Combination." Show a transparency of at least one of the combination resumes from pages 10 and 11. Ask the following question:

- *"Why is the combination resume the most flexible and informative of the three resume types we have discussed?"* (Answer: A combination resume lets you list all your related skills, experiences, and work history.)

Give the students time to complete their three-column chart and place it in their **blue folders**.

Have a student read aloud "Resume Power Words" on page 12. Be sure to define any power words that the students find unclear or confusing. Follow with **Activity #1** (see page 129).

Choose several categories to display on the board/overhead. The following diagram shows an example of how this could look (see page 137 for a transparency master):

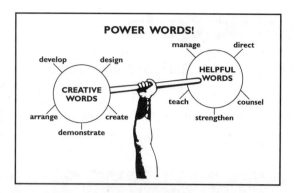

Tell the students to copy these categories and titles onto the back of their **blue folders.**

Complete **Think About It** on pages 13–18. When the students have finished this section, have them pull it out and place it in their **blue folders.**

Have a student read aloud "Tailor Your Resume: Different Resumes for Different Jobs" on page 19. Ask the following question:

- *"Why not have an all-purpose resume and use it to apply for all jobs?"* (Answer: The skills and experience sections should reflect the type of job you're applying for. You don't need to include skills and experience that aren't related to the job.)

Have the students look at pages 20 and 21, "Resume Questions and Answers." Ask the class for 14 volunteers. Divide these volunteers into seven pairs. Assign each pair one of the questions on pages 20 and 21. Explain that the pairs will read the question and answer they have been assigned. Then they will decide how to present the question and answer to the entire class. They may role-play a late-night interview segment, a television commercial, or a friendly conversation, or they can create a visual display that states and answers the question assigned to them.

If the class has a few more than 14 students, the groups can have three people so that the whole class is involved. If the class has many more than 14 students, assign each question and answer to two different groups and present each question and answer twice.

Tell the students to pull out the sample resumes at the end of this chapter and put them in their **blue folders** to keep them safe so they can refer to them later.

Quick Quiz

Name: _____

Directions: *Complete the crossword puzzle. The answers are vocabulary words from chapter 1.*

Across

5. Skill or experience needed for the job

6. Summary of skills and experience on paper

Down

1. A form you fill out when you apply for a job

2. Emphasize certain experience on your resume

3. Making your resume fit the job

4. The employer calls these people to verify your employment history

Quick Quiz Answer Key

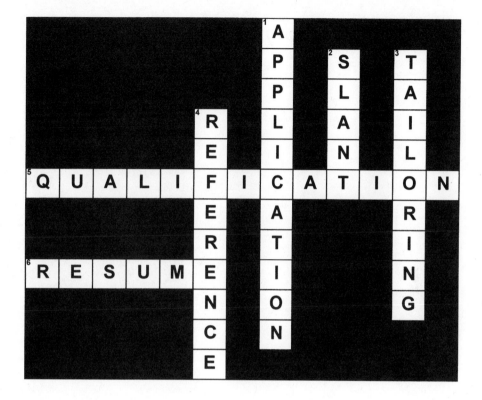

The crossword puzzle answers:

1. APPLICATION (down)
2. SLAN (down)
3. TAILORING (down)
4. REFERENCE (down)
5. QUALIFICATION (across)
6. RESUME (across)

Think On This...

- Have you ever filled out a job application?

- What do you remember about it?

- Was it easy to fill out?

- What information did you need to have in order to fill it out completely?

- Did you get the job you filled out the application for?

- If you did, great! If you did not, do you think the application was part of the problem?

- Think about ways you could prepare to fill out job applications and make a list in your mind.

Job Applications

CHAPTER OBJECTIVES

1. To understand the purpose of applications.

2. To learn the best way to fill out applications.

3. To create an inventory of information that can be used on applications.

4. To practice filling out applications.

Working Vocabulary

- **Abbreviation.** A shortened form of a longer word is an *abbreviation*.

- **Salary.** The amount of money that a job pays per year is the *salary*. (If the job pays by the hour, the money is sometimes referred to as *wages*.)

- **Marital status.** The state of being married or unmarried is called *marital status*.

- **Dependents.** Children or other people who need you for financial support are your *dependents*.

- **Supervisor.** The person who is responsible for hiring, training, and disciplining you is your *supervisor*.

- **Network.** A *network* is a group of people who can tell you about jobs or job openings.

- **Anticipate.** You *anticipate* when you look ahead and plan for what might happen in the future.

- **Acquire.** *Acquire* means to learn or to get.

- **Monitor.** When something is watched to see what it does or where it goes, it is *monitored*.

- **Allocate.** Distributing items among a group is to *allocate* them.

Presentation Suggestions

Begin by reading **Think On This...** from the end of chapter 1. Ask the students to share some of their thoughts about the topic, as well as some of their experiences with job applications. Then read the **Chapter Objectives** for chapter 2. Ask the students to discuss how **Think On This...** from chapter 1 relates to the **Chapter Objectives** from chapter 2. Next, read the **Working Vocabulary**. Add the words for chapter 2 to the running list. Explain that many of the words are words that might be found on job applications.

Ask a student to read aloud "What Is an Application?" and "Why Employers Use Applications" from page 28.

Introduce the letters *N P C.* Explain that the students should keep these three letters in mind when filling out job applications, because each letter stands for a rule to follow when filling out job applications. The rules are as follows:

- Be Neat.

- Have a Positive attitude.

- Make sure the application is Complete.

The following diagram shows how these rules will look on the board/overhead (see page 138 for a transparency master):

N-P-C
(rules to follow)

1) be **N**eat!
2) have a **P**ositive attitude!
3) make sure the application is **C**omplete.

WHAT DO THESE SAY ABOUT YOU?

The students might want to remember the three letters by making up a sentence in which each word of the sentence begins with one of those letters, such as Nine People Called. Suggest that students write the rules and the sentences they made up for remembering them on their **blue folders.**

Choose a student to read aloud page 29, "Preparation: What You Need to Fill Out an Application." When the student is done, ask the following questions:

- *"What should you use to fill out an application?"* (Answer: An erasable black pen.)

- *"Why should you not use a pencil?"* (Answer: It looks messy when erased, and pencil can smudge and be hard to read.)

- *"How many applications should you pick up?"* (Answer: Take two in case you make mistakes.)

- *"Why might you want to fill out the application before leaving the place of employment?"* (Answer: The employer will know that no one else helped you fill it out.)

Ask another student to read aloud "Your Application Inventory, Section I—Personal Information" at the top of page 30. Review the definition of *inventory* before beginning the written sections. Have a student find the sentence on the page that gives the definition of *inventory*. (Answer: An *inventory* is an organized collection of information.) Allow time for the students to complete pages 30–38 (top). Be available to answer the students' questions.

When most of the students have finished these pages, repeat and answer any questions that were voiced by more than one student. Write several of the most common questions and the answers on the board/overhead. Then read, discuss, and have the students complete **Think About It** on pages 38–39.

Choose someone to read aloud "Power Words for Applications" on pages 40 and 41. Follow with **Activity #1.**

Move on to "Inventory Section II—Employment Information" at the bottom of page 41. Read the directions to the class. Then ask a student to reread the directions to make sure everyone knows what to do. Have the students complete pages 42–48. Be available to answer any questions students might have as they complete these pages. Stop and write any common questions on the board/overhead with the answers. Next, have the students complete **Think About It** on pages 49–50.

Proceed with the directions for "Inventory Section III—Education and Training Information." Read the directions aloud. Then ask a student to reread the directions. Continue with completing pages 51–54, answering questions as before, writing common questions and answers on the board/overhead. Have the students complete **Think About It** on pages 55–56.

Choose a student to read aloud "Inventory Section IV—References" and "What Is a Reference?" on page 57. Ask the students to find any **Working Vocabulary** words in the text of page 57. Review the definitions of those words (*reference, networking*).

Read the directions for "Inventory Section V—References Information" on page 58. Have the students complete the **References Worksheet** on pages 58–65. Next, tell the students to complete **Think About It** on pages 65–66.

Have the students pull out each of the inventory sections and put them in their **blue folders.** This way, all the information will be easy to find when they are filling out applications on their own. They could even take the folder with them when they fill out applications at places of employment.

Copy pages 67, 68, 70, and 71 as overhead transparencies so they are easy to view. Show page 67 first, and then page 68. Ask the questions on the next page.

- *"What do you think of this person just from looking at his application? Can you tell anything about him based only on the application?"* (Accept any appropriate responses.)

- *"Can you identify Albert's mistakes?"*

List their answers on the board/overhead. Then show pages 70 and 71. Ask the following question:

- *"What do you think of this person based only on his application?"*

Next, turn to page 69 and see how many of the 21 things the class found when they looked at pages 67 and 68. Compare pages 67 and 68 to pages 70 and 71.

Tell the students to turn to pages 72–81. Explain that they will be choosing one of the sample applications to fill out as best they can in class. Tell the students to pull out the rest of the applications and put them in their **blue folders** so that they will have them for future practice.

Think On This...

- What do you think a cover letter is? Do you already know?

- Why do you think you might write one?

- Speaking of letters, have you ever heard of a follow-up letter?

- All of these things have something to do with applying for jobs, so all of them have to do with your finding a job!

- If you had to write a letter to someone explaining why you are the best person for a job, what would you say to that person to make him or her want to meet you in person?

Chapter Three

Cover Letters and Follow-Up Letters

CHAPTER OBJECTIVES

1. To learn what a cover letter is used for.

2. To see what goes into a cover letter.

3. To practice writing a cover letter.

4. To learn what a follow-up letter is used for.

5. To see what goes into a follow-up letter.

6. To practice writing a follow-up letter.

Working Vocabulary

● **Cover letter.** A *cover letter* is a letter written to a potential employer and that is included with an application or resume. It states qualifications and reasons to hire an applicant.

● **Follow-up letter.** A letter that is sent to remind a potential employer who you are, restate your interest in a job, ask whether the job has been filled yet, or thank someone for an interview is a *follow-up letter.*

Presentation Suggestions

Reread **Think On This...** from the end of chapter 2. Discuss the students' responses to **Think On This....** Then ask them to guess what the objectives for chapter 3 will be. Write these on the board/overhead. Next, present the actual **Chapter Objectives** for chapter 3. Allow time for the students to compare their guesses to the actual objectives.

Add the two new **Working Vocabulary** words to the lists from chapters 1 and 2. Take some time to review all the vocabulary words.

Choose a student to read "What Is a Cover Letter?" and "When Should You Write Cover Letters?" on page 84. Ask the following questions:

● *"Why is a cover letter necessary if you have already listed your qualifications for a job in a resume or on an application?"* (Answer: It communicates a tone of personal warmth and convinces an employer to look at your resume and invite you in for an interview.)

● *"How often do you need to write a new cover letter?"* (Answer: Every time you apply for a job.)

● *"What do you do if you do not know the name of the person to whom you are writing the letter?"* (Answer: Try your best to find out the person's name. If you can't, address it to "Dear Sir or Madam" or "To the owner/manager of _____ .")

Give each student a 4 × 6 index card. On the blank side, have them write COVER LETTERS. Then have a student read aloud "What Goes in a Cover Letter?" on page 85. As the student reads the section, tell the students to write anything they want to remember about a cover letter on the index card. When the reading is done, ask the students to share some of the things they have written. Write these on the board/overhead so that the students can add them to their cards if they want to.

Call on a student to read aloud "Basic Cover Letter Tips" on page 86. Use a board/overhead display such as the following to focus their attention (see page 139 for a transparency master):

> **COVER LETTER TIPS:**
>
> 1) Must be typed.
> 2) Use 8½ by 11-inch stationery.
> 3) Keep it short; 2 to 3 paragraphs.
> 4) Show you have the skills required.
> 5) Say things that relate to the employer's needs, not your own!
> 6) Sell relevant accomplishments.
> 7) Mention someone you know who works for the company, IF they are well thought of by the employers.

Use transparency copies of pages 87 and 88 to start a discussion about the information. Then have the students complete the **Challenge** on pages 89–91.

Review the definition of the term *follow-up letter.* Then ask a student to read "Follow-Up Letters" and "Are Follow-Up Letters Really Useful?" on page 92. When the student has finished reading the sections, ask the following questions:

- *"How long should you wait to send a follow-up letter?"* (Answer: A couple of weeks.)

- *"When is a follow-up letter used as a thank-you letter?"* (Answer: When it is sent after an interview.)

- *What is the purpose of a follow-up letter?"* (Answer: To remind the employer who you are, to restate interest in the job, to ask whether the job has been filled, or to say thank you for their time.)

Ask a student to read aloud "Is It Okay to Call Instead of Writing?" on page 93. When the student has finished reading the section, ask the following question:

- *"What should you say to a potential employer if you decide to make a follow-up phone call?"* (Answer: Ask whether the employer has had a chance to look at your resume/application yet, and is it possible to set up an interview?)

Follow this question with **Activity #2** (see page 131).

Create transparencies of pages 94 and 95. Direct the students' attention to these and the corresponding pages in their books. Start a discussion about these examples, and answer any student questions. Show how each follow-up letter goes with the cover letter sent by the same person earlier in the chapter. Ask the following questions:

- *"Why did Cynthia Roberts send a follow-up letter?"* (Answer: Because she sent a resume two weeks earlier and had not gotten a response.)

- *"Why did Reggie Rudolph send a follow-up letter?"* (Answer: To thank the employer for an interview and to reemphasize why he would be a good person to hire.)

Then have the students complete **Challenge** on pages 96–98. Take the time to talk about any common problems that the students might be having during the writing process.

Activity #1

Groups and Categories

FORMAT: Small group

TIME: 15–20 minutes

MATERIALS: Word lists from page 12, scissors, pens/pencils, paper

1. Assign the students to groups of three or four.

2. Using photocopies of the words on pages 40–41, have the students work together to cut the words apart and form as many separate groups of words as they can think of by grouping them according to any common theme. (If possible, you can cut apart the words before class starts. You can then give the words to the students in envelopes.)

3. The students can move the individual words around to help them visualize the groupings.

4. The words can be used in more than one group.

5. Here are some examples:

Helpful Words

- assist
- direct
- manage
- counsel
- strengthen
- teach

Words About Education

- test
- train
- report
- teach

Words for Planning Ahead

- anticipate
- prepare
- monitor
- direct
- progress
- furnish
- promote
- plan
- schedule

Creative Words

- develop
- demonstrate
- make
- upgrade
- stimulate
- assemble

Words That Show Action

- accept
- control
- give
- secure
- strengthen
- acquire
- develop
- execute
- monitor
- supervise
- arrange
- exercise
- organize
- review
- analyze
- contribute
- identify

People Words

- teach
- encourage
- review
- train
- decide

Interaction Words

- determine
- meet
- test
- consider
- select
- contact
- counsel
- handle
- recommend
- promote
- encourage

6. Each word group must contain at least three words and a theme title.

7. Ask several groups to share their word groups and categories with the entire class.

Activity #2

Role-Play It

FORMAT: Paired

TIME: 25–30 minutes

MATERIALS: Photocopies of pages 92–93, pens/pencils, paper, cards with the words "good example" or "poor example" written on them

1. Group the students into pairs.

2. Ask one partner to choose a card.

3. Explain that the card tells the team what kind of follow-up example they will role-play.

4. Ask the team to create a script for a follow-up call or letter. If the team chooses to do a written example, they will need to be ready to read their letters aloud. The class will respond by showing the reaction the employer might have toward that potential employee.

5. Have fun with these examples.

Comprehensive Vocabulary Quiz for Book 3

JOB SEARCH TOOLS: RESUMES, APPLICATIONS, AND COVER LETTERS

Name: _____

Directions: *Fill in the blank with the correct word from the word-search puzzle list. After you have filled in the blanks, find the words in the puzzle.*

1. When you make your resume fit a certain job, you are _____ it to the employer's needs.

2. You might have to fill out an _____ and send a resume for some jobs.

3. Your _____ tells people whether you are married or single.

4. The _____ of people you know might be able to help you find a job or point you in the right direction.

5. The amount of money a job pays per year is the _____ .

6. You might have a _____ or a boss or both at your next job.

7. Never use these shortened words, or _____ , on an application.

8. You might _____ skills that will help you in a job during school or other training.

9. A _____ is a more personal way of telling an employer that you have the interest and the qualifications for a job.

10. Be sure to ask anyone you use as a _____ whether a potential employer can call them at home or work.

11. A _____ may list experience or education and may be in functional or chronological format.

12. Be sure to _____ the classified ads to see what jobs are open.

13. At a previous job, you might have had to _____ time among several different tasks.

14. It will help if you can _____ problems before they happen.

15. Your children are the most common type of _____ , because they count on you for money.

16. Employers will be impressed if you _____ with a phone call or a thank-you note.

17. A skill that is specifically required by an employer in order to be considered for a job is a _____ .

18. When you _____ your resume, you emphasize certain areas of experience more than others.

S	T	N	E	D	N	E	P	E	D	X	N	S	M	U
Y	U	E	B	U	B	R	O	T	I	N	O	M	E	X
S	M	T	R	K	U	Y	R	A	K	W	I	C	R	O
E	C	R	A	B	B	R	E	V	I	A	T	I	O	N
T	N	O	I	T	A	C	I	F	I	L	A	U	Q	E
A	A	S	V	T	S	E	I	F	B	N	C	O	H	T
C	C	I	E	E	M	L	O	X	T	N	I	P	P	W
O	Q	V	L	U	R	L	A	I	W	B	L	O	O	O
L	U	R	S	O	L	L	C	T	T	I	P	V	Q	R
L	I	E	F	O	R	I	E	K	I	N	P	D	F	K
A	R	P	W	Z	P	I	K	T	Y	R	A	L	A	S
I	E	U	O	A	Q	D	N	G	T	C	A	L	G	H
S	P	S	T	C	J	B	K	G	H	E	M	M	S	R
L	H	E	C	N	E	R	E	F	E	R	R	O	S	X

abbreviation

acquire

allocate

anticipate

application

cover letter

dependents

follow up

marital status

monitor

network

qualification

reference

resume

salary

slant

supervisor

tailoring

Answer Key

1. tailoring
2. application
3. marital status
4. network
5. salary
6. supervisor
7. abbreviations
8. acquire
9. cover letter

10. reference
11. resume
12. monitor
13. allocate
14. anticipate
15. dependents
16. follow up
17. qualification
18. slant

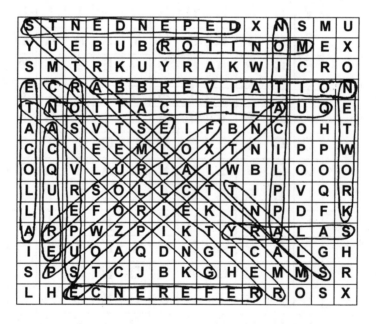

From chapter 1, page 113

RESUME ITEMS

NAME	ADDRESS	PHONE — DAY / EVENING
JOB OBJECTIVES	QUALIFICATIONS	
EDUCATION	REFERENCES	WORK EXPERIENCE

From chapter 1, page 113

TYPES OF RESUMES

FUNCTIONAL	COMBINATION	CHRONOLOGICAL

POWER WORDS!

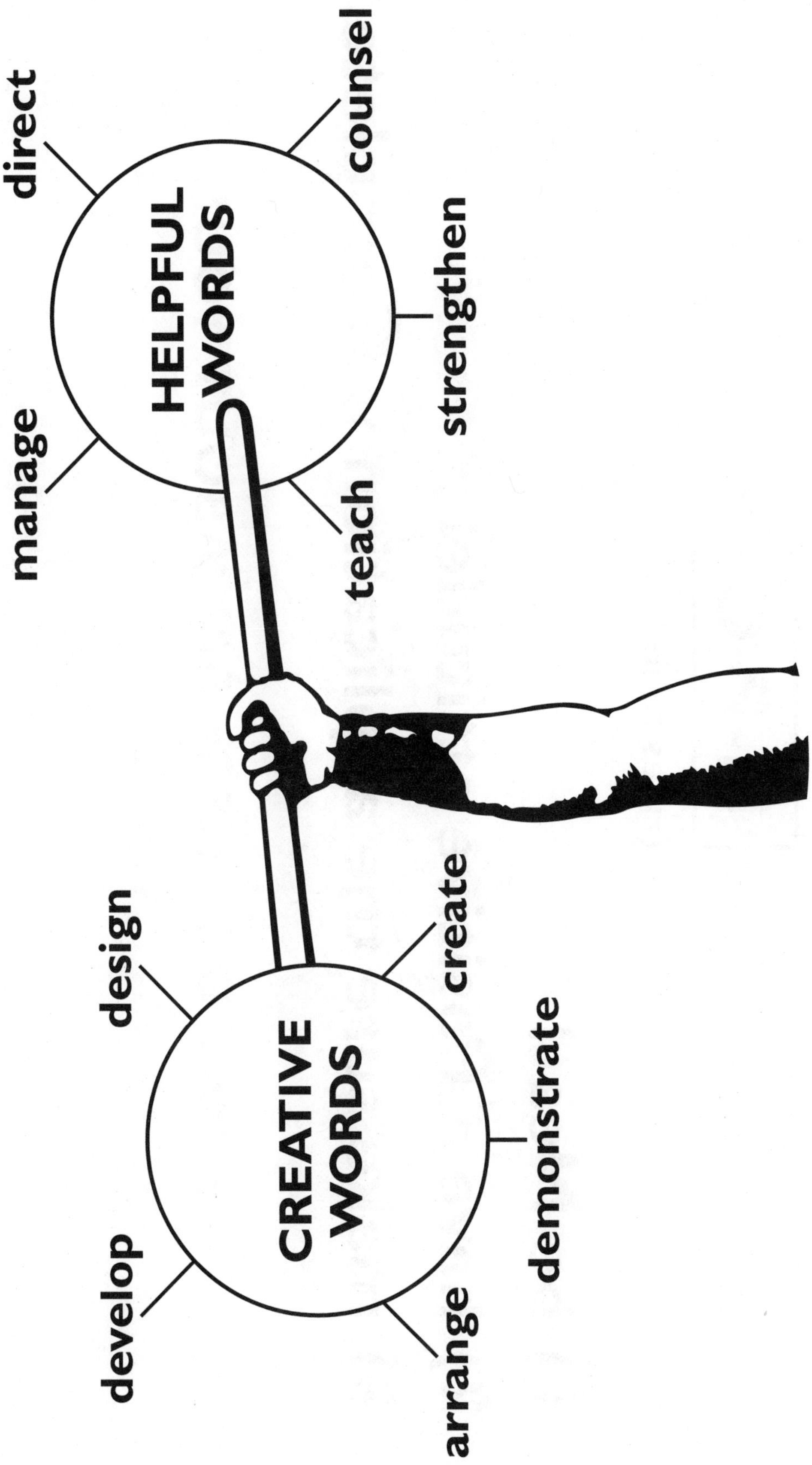

HELPFUL WORDS

direct

counsel

strengthen

manage

teach

CREATIVE WORDS

design

create

develop

demonstrate

arrange

© 2000 • JIST Works • Indianapolis

N-P-C

(rules to follow)

1) be **N**eat!

2) have a **P**ositive attitude!

3) make sure the application is **C**omplete.

WHAT DO THESE SAY ABOUT YOU?

COVER LETTER TIPS:

1) Must be typed.

2) Use 8½ by 11-inch stationery.

3) Keep it short; 2 to 3 paragraphs.

4) Show you have the skills required.

5) Say things that relate to the employer's needs, not your own!

6) Sell relevant accomplishments.

7) Mention someone you know who works for the company, IF they are well thought of by the employers.

PART IV

Instructor's Resources for

NETWORKING AND INTERVIEWING FOR JOBS

Workbook Table of Contents

Networking and Interviewing for Jobs

Your Most Essential Job Search Tool— Your Personal Network

CHAPTER OBJECTIVES

1. To learn what a network is and why a network is important.

2. To build a strong network.

3. To learn how to use a network to get leads and referrals.

Working Vocabulary

- **Network.** The people you know and the people they know are your *network*.

- **Networking.** Using word of mouth to find jobs is *networking*.

- **Hidden job market.** Jobs that are not advertised in classified ads, employment agencies, or anywhere else are part of the *hidden job market*.

- **Job lead.** Information about a possible job opening is called a *job lead*.

- **Service organization.** Any organization that provides a service for others, often on a volunteer basis, is a *service organization*.

- **Referral.** The name of somebody specific to talk to—someone a friend or an acquaintance knows personally—is a *referral*.

Presentation Suggestions

Begin the first chapter by introducing the **Working Vocabulary** words individually. Use a chalkboard, overhead, or chart paper to keep a continuing display in the classroom. Add each chapter's vocabulary words to the list for display. Be sure to review the words with the students a second time as they appear in the text. Be certain that the students are familiar with the words and their definitions.

Introduce the **Chapter Objectives.** These will focus the students on the tasks at hand. List the objectives on the board/overhead at the beginning of the chapter. Then check them off as the class progresses, or at the end of the chapter, just as if it were a grocery list or to-do list.

Ask a student to read page 4, "What Is a Network and Why Do You Need One?" Clarify the definitions of *network, hidden job market,* and *cold-calling* as they appear in the text. Ask another student to read "How Do You Use a Network?" at the bottom of page 4.

Use the following diagram to illustrate the idea of a network and how it works (see page 181 for a transparency master):

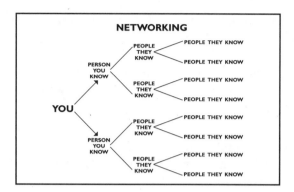

Follow with **Activity #1** (see page 172).

Ask another student to read aloud "Who Is in Your Network?" on page 5. Brainstorm with the class about where to find people to add to a network. Use the following diagram (see page 182 for a transparency master), putting the names of people to contact in the blank circles with suggestions from students. Examples they might supply include friends, teachers, landlords, and so on.

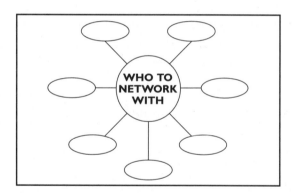

Discuss the directions for completing **Think About It** on pages 5–11. Then allow time for the class to complete the assignment.

Move on to **Think About It** on pages 12–13. Ask a student to read the text aloud. When finished, allow time for the students to write their responses. Then invite several pairs of students to use their responses to role-play the conversations.

Invite a student to read aloud "Use Your Network to Build a Bigger Network" on page 14. When they have finished reading, ask the following questions:

- *"What is a network?"* (Answer: The people you know and the people they know.)

- *"Why is it important to build a network?"* (Answer: A network is important because it gives you a group of people who are willing and able to help you in a job search.)

- *"How should you approach people who you think might be able to become part of your network?"* (Answer: Be friendly, respectful, and appreciative of their support and assistance.)

Have another student read "Volunteer Your Time As a Way of Building Your Network" on page 14. Ask the following question:

- *"How can volunteering help you even though you won't be paid for a volunteer job?"* (Answer: It can give you more connections to add to your network or give you an advantage if you think you might want to apply for a paid position with the same organization.)

Allow time for the students to complete **Think About It** on page 15. If time allows, ask the students to share their suggestions for volunteer work with the entire class. In this way, the students will be able to build their lists even further.

Give each student a **yellow folder.** The students may write their volunteer work suggestions on the front of the folder in bold print to keep them in a place that's easy to remember. The students may also want to add to their folders the networking pages they completed earlier.

Ask a student to read aloud "Leads and Referrals" on page 16. Review the vocabulary words used on page 16. Ask for two student volunteers to read the conversations between Don and Mike in the **Example** on pages 16 and 17. Ask the class to suggest how Mike might use the network and referrals he receives from Don. Next, ask the students to continue reading "Special Networking Tip: Sometimes You Can Turn Leads into Referrals."

Tell the students to complete **Checkpoint** on pages 18–19. Review the answers with them when they are done.

Checkpoint Answers

1. The people you know and the people they know.

2. A network gives you a group of people who are willing and able to help you in your job search.

3. Friends, neighbors, relatives, teachers, and so on.

4. Doing volunteer work; talking to people and asking them for the names of others who might help; joining a church.

5. A lead is someone who knows about a job opening; a referral is having a personal connection to a job opening.

6. A referral is more important, because it provides a personal connection to a specific organization or company.

Think On This...

You have just discussed networking and how you can use it to help you in your search for a job. Now think about what cold-calling means.

- Are you ready to call places you might be interested in working, even if you don't know anyone there?

- What will you say that will make those people want to talk to you again in person?

- Can you handle it if your call is blocked by a receptionist?

- What if the employer does not want to even talk to you?

- How will you prepare yourself for this next challenge?

Tap the Hidden Job Market Through Cold-Calling

CHAPTER OBJECTIVES

1. To learn what cold-calling is and why it is important.

2. To learn how to use the yellow pages to find businesses and companies to cold-call.

3. To practice using phone scripts and learning how to get past "screeners."

4. To learn about the other cold-calling technique: just "dropping in."

Working Vocabulary

- **Cold-calling.** Making direct contact with an employer you have never met or spoken with before, who has not advertised for help, without having been referred to them, is *cold-calling*.

- **Potential.** Anything that has the possibility or promise of something yet to happen has *potential*.

- **Screener.** The receptionist or secretary who guards the time and privacy of the person who does the hiring is the *screener*.

- **Script.** A *script* is a written version of what is to be said, word for word.

Presentation Suggestions

Begin chapter 2 by reviewing the **Think On This...** from the end of chapter 1. Discuss the students' responses and explain that they will be referring to their ideas throughout the chapter.

Then present the **Working Vocabulary** words for chapter 2. Add these words to the displayed list from chapter 1. Be sure to include both the words and the definitions in the display. The more the students see the words, the more they will recognize and use them in their daily life.

Introduce the chapter 2 **Chapter Objectives**. Again, write these on the board/overhead and check off each one as it is discussed or at the end of the chapter. Keep the objectives visible throughout the chapter's lessons to provide focus and a sense of accomplishment.

Ask a student volunteer to read aloud "What Is Cold-Calling?", "Why Bother Cold-Calling?", and "Your Goal: Getting an Interview" on page 22. When the student has finished reading, ask the following questions:

- *"What is cold-calling?"* (Answer: Making direct contact with an employer you have never met, spoken with, or been referred to.)

- *"Why might cold-calling be difficult?"* (Answer: It might make you nervous to talk about a job to people you don't know.)

- *"What is the actual goal of cold-calling?"* (Answer: Getting an interview.)

Ask a student to read aloud "Use the Yellow Pages" on page 23. When the student has finished reading, ask the following question:

- *"In which section of the yellow pages should you begin looking for potential employers?"* (Answer: The index section.)

Proceed directly to the directions for "Use the Yellow Pages Index" on page 23. Read aloud the directions to the class, and then ask a student to read the directions again. Read each section of text on pages 24–26 aloud to the students. Stop after each section to give the students time to fill in their answers. Review the students' answers for this section, answer any questions, and identify any common problems the students might have had with using the index.

Call on another student to read aloud the **Example** on page 26. Next, give each student a sheet of lined paper and a pencil or pen. Use either the yellow pages index on page 24 or an actual copy of the yellow pages. Allow about 15 minutes for the students to begin compiling a list of potential employers in the same manner that Maria did in the example. (Note: If your institution's rules prevent inmates from having phone books, consider this exercise optional.)

Invite a student to read "Get Even More Leads" on page 27. If the class was able to begin a listing of potential employers using the yellow pages, allow 5–10 minutes for the students to use the "1, 2, 3" method on their own lists. Have the students place these lists in their **yellow folders.**

Ask a student to read aloud "Get Past the 'Screeners'" on pages 27–28. Ask the following questions:

- *"What information should you give to a screener?"* (Answer: As little as possible.)

- *"Give an example of how you might treat a screener as an expert about the company."* (Answer: Ask who is the best person to talk to about something, or ask a few questions about the company.)

Ask for several student volunteers to read the **Example** on pages 29–30 in parts. After each section, discuss with the class what happened, and have the students suggest how they think Maria could get past the screener. See if any of the students' suggestions appear in the final section of the script, when Maria is finally successful.

Read aloud the text at the bottom of page 30. Ask the following questions:

- *"What are two key words to help you get past a screener?"* (Answer: Indirect and creative. Ask the students for examples of both of these.)

- *"How long should you wait to call back if you were stopped by a screener?"* (Answer: At least a week.)

Have a student read aloud "Telephone Scripts" on pages 31–32. Follow with **Activity #2** (see page 173). Remember to leave some time for open discussion of both the scenes from the activity and the preceding information.

Continue by having the students complete **Think About It** on pages 32–33. You could also incorporate this page into **Activity #2** if there is not enough time to do both.

Read aloud the text "Practice Phone Scripts with Friends" on page 34. Then ask two students to role-play the **Example** conversation on pages 34–35. Ask a third student to read the text that comes before and after the conversation.

Proceed directly to "Worksheet: Your Job Prospects Notebook" at the bottom of page 35. The students will not be able to complete this in class. They should staple together the entire section (pages 36–39) and place it in their **yellow folders.** They will use these sheets later when they are actually doing their cold-calling. Be certain that they know how to use this section and why it is important to keep track of the calls they have made, as well as the results of the calls.

Have a student volunteer read "Just Drop In" on pages 40–41. Ask the following questions:

- *"What is the difference between dropping in and cold-calling?"* (Answer: Just dropping in happens in person; cold-calling refers to using a phone.)

- *"Which is more effective?"* (Answer: It depends upon the employer.)

If you're using an overhead projector, enlarge and copy the JIST Card® example on page 42 onto a transparency sheet. Place the transparency on the overhead so that it is easy for the students to see. Have a student read aloud "Uses of a JIST Card" at the bottom of page 42. Explain to the students that a JIST Card is like a mini-resume. It is easy to carry along on drop-in visits and easy to attach to applications and resumes. You can also give it to the people in your network.

Give each student an index card. Ask them to copy the elements of a JIST Card in the order they appear in the example. Then allow a few minutes for the students to fill in at least part of the card with their personal information. Have them put these in their **yellow folders.**

Read aloud "Follow Up and Call Back" on page 43. When finished, ask the following question:

- *"Why should you follow up even if you did not get an interview?"* (Answer: To let the employer know you appreciate his or her time and are still interested in a job with the company.)

Have the students complete **Checkpoint** on pages 43–44. Discuss the answers with the students when they have finished.

Checkpoint Answers

1. Contact with an employer you have not met, spoken to, or been referred to, and who has not advertised a job opening.

2. The goal of cold-calling is to get an interview.

3. Screeners are people (usually receptionists) who protect the time and privacy of the person who does the hiring. You have to be indirect and creative to get past a good screener. You might have to try several times before you are successful.

4. You can make a telephone script and practice for a cold call.

5. Dropping in on a potential employer allows the employer to see you in person and talk to you. He or she might get a better idea of the kind of person you are.

6. Cold-calling by telephone is a bit less scary and gives you a way to make an impression that both you and the employer are prepared for.

7. Following up lets the employer know that you appreciated his time. It reminds him of who you are and that you are still interested in a job. Following up with the people in your network reminds them that you are still looking for a job, and gives you a chance to tell them about your skills again.

Quick Quiz

Name: _____

Directions: *Complete the following crossword puzzle. The answers are vocabulary words from chapters 1 and 2.*

Across

1. Call or visit an employer unannounced

6. Hidden _____ ; jobs that aren't advertised

7. Someone specific to talk to about job leads

8. Possibility

9. What you will say

Down

2. Service _____ ; a group that can help you

3. Finding jobs by word of mouth

4. Tip about where to look for jobs

5. Receptionist

Quick Quiz Answer Key

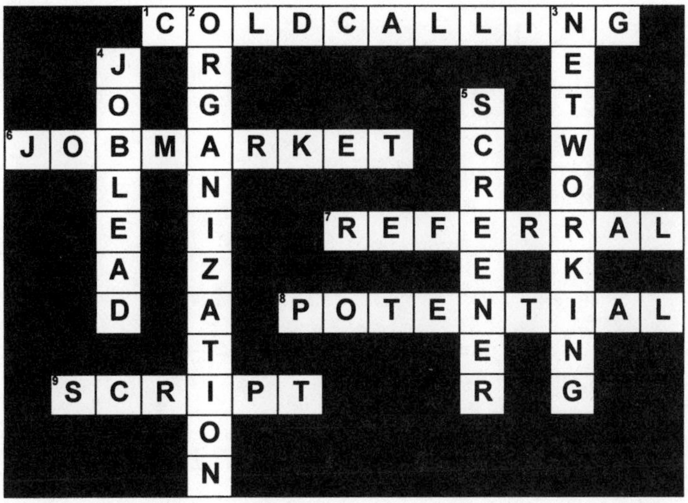
COLDCALLING
ORGANIZATION
NETWORKING
JOBLEAD
SCREENER
JOBMARKET
REFERRAL
POTENTIAL
SCRIPT

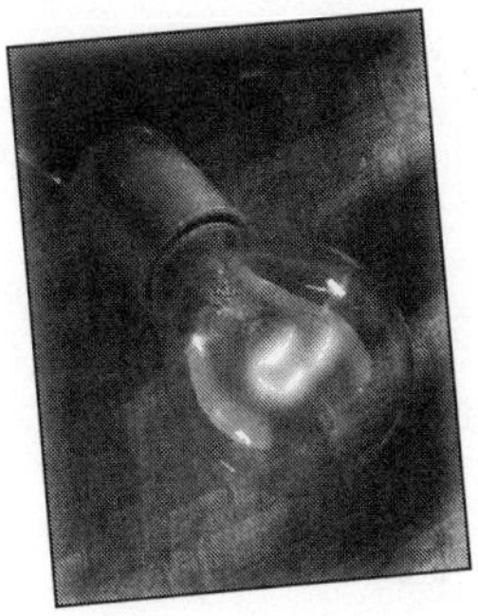

Think On This...

If your cold-calling works well, you will have more than one interview to prepare for.

- What will you do to impress the potential employer?
- What questions should you expect to be asked?
- Is there anything you can think of that you might want to bring with you?
- How should you dress for an interview?

All these things could be the difference between becoming employed and being turned away.

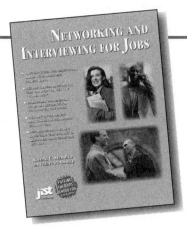

Chapter Three

Prepare for the Interview

CHAPTER OBJECTIVES

1. To learn what you should know before going to an interview.

2. To learn what to expect in an interview.

3. To learn what you should bring to an interview.

4. To learn about dressing and grooming for an interview.

Working Vocabulary

- **Interview.** A meeting with someone to discuss a job opening is an *interview*.

- **Occupation.** An *occupation* is another word for a job.

- **Advancement.** The ability to move forward and progress in your job is *advancement*.

- **Promotion.** A *promotion* is a move up in salary and responsibility, usually given to you when you do good work.

- **Document.** A piece of paper containing official information is a *document*. Your resume is an example of a *document*.

Presentation Suggestions

Begin by reviewing the **Think On This...** section from the end of chapter 2. Reread the questions and allow time for the students to respond. If the students have answered the questions in written form, they will need to have their responses in front of them. If they are answering orally, you will need to repeat the questions several times or display them on the board/overhead.

Next, ask the students to guess what some of the **Chapter Objectives** for this chapter might be, based on the topics from **Think On This....** The students should be able to recognize that there is a connection between the sections. If they do not respond quickly, review the **Think On This...** sections and **Chapter Objectives** from previous chapters and demonstrate the thought process that connects them—that **Think On This...** is a preview of the topics that will be covered in the next chapter. Then post the actual **Chapter Objectives** so that the students can see how close their "guesses" are.

Display the **Working Vocabulary** words for chapter 3. Review both the pronunciations and the definitions, adding them to the lists from the previous chapters. This will also give you a chance to review *all* the **Working Vocabulary** words presented so far.

Keeping the **Chapter Objectives** and **Working Vocabulary** on the board/overhead, ask a student to read aloud page 46, "Arm Yourself with Knowledge." Allow time for the students to write the three kinds of knowledge they will need in an interview on the front of their **yellow folders.** Use the diagram on the next page while students are reading pages 46–48 (see page 183 for a transparency master).

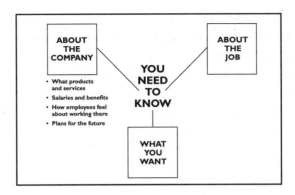

Ask a student volunteer to read aloud "Knowledge of the Company" on page 46. Discuss the places where you can find information about a specific company. Add the heading "Information Sources" to the diagram, under "About the Company," and list the sources.

Have another student read aloud "Knowledge of the Job" on page 47. Follow the same procedure as in the preceding paragraph to discuss and display relevant information. Continue with reading page 48, "Knowledge of What *You* Want." Then give each student three 4 × 6 index cards and have them copy the condensed information from the board/overhead onto the three separate cards. These will be placed in the students' **yellow folders.**

Have the students complete **Think About It** on pages 48–49 individually. Review the correct answers as a class.

Direct the students' attention to "Questions to Expect" on page 50. Read each question aloud. After you read each question, allow a student to answer it as if they were in an interview. Ask the others in the class to "rate" the person's response. Ask the following questions:

- *"How do you think _____ answered the question?"*

- *"Is there anything you would add to or delete from their response?"*

Allow time for discussion. Then ask the following question:

- *"Did you think that was a fair question?"*

There will be varying answers to this, but accept any appropriate responses in favor of both fair and unfair. Have the students explain why they think a question is fair or unfair. Then read aloud the text at the top of page 51.

Choose two students to read "Basic Interview Principles" on page 51. After each bullet point is read, ask a sample question (see below). Call on one or two students to answer the question. Discuss their responses as a group. Offer examples of how you can change certain answers to better answers without lying.

After the first bullet point, ask the following question:

- *"What are the best qualities you will bring to our company, and how will you use those skills?"*

After the second bullet point, ask the following question:

- *"If you are hired, what are your goals for the future?"*

After the third bullet point, ask the following question:

- *"Have you worked in a team setting? Describe the experience."*

Invite a student volunteer to read aloud "Questions to Take with You" on pages 52–53. Explain that an employer often likes to know that an interviewee is interested enough in the job to have prepared a few questions. After the student has read this section, give each student an index card on which to copy the questions at the bottom of page 52. Have the students put these cards in their **yellow folders**.

Have a student read aloud "Questions Not to Ask" on page 53. Discuss the reasons why these types of questions are not appropriate for an interview situation.

Allow the student to continue reading "Role-Playing" at the bottom of page 53. Follow with **Activity #3** (see page 174).

Discuss employment testing with the class. First, ask the students how many different types of tests they have taken. Then discuss the fact that sometimes an interviewer requires a test of some sort. Testing will not be a part of every interview, but it might be used in some cases, especially for a specialized job that requires specific knowledge. Ask a student to then read aloud "Taking Employment Tests" and "Test Tips" on pages 54–55.

Have a student read aloud "Personal Grooming" on pages 55–56. Discuss the section as a class. Be prepared to answer any questions the students might have about this section and what is expected.

Use the following diagram to display the information from page 57 in an organized manner (see page 184 for a transparency master):

BRING THESE TO AN INTERVIEW!

* RESUME
* DRIVER'S LICENSE
* MILITARY RECORDS
* SCHOOL CERTIFICATES
* BIRTH CERTIFICATE
* SOCIAL SECURITY CARD
* LETTERS OF RECOMMENDATION
* U.S. COAST GUARD MERCHANT MARINER CARD

* UNION CARD
* DIPLOMA
* SCHOOL ID CARD
* NOTEPAD
* PEN

Give each student a 4 × 6 index card to copy the board/overhead display. Have the students put the cards in their **yellow folders.**

Ask a student to read aloud the two paragraphs at the bottom of page 57. Add the things mentioned in the paragraphs to the list on the board/overhead.

Have the students complete **Think About It** on page 58 individually. Discuss the answers as a group.

Invite a student volunteer to read aloud page 59, "Relax!" Discuss the importance of being relaxed and confident in an interview. Proceed by having another student read aloud "Going to the Interview" on page 60.

Next, have the students complete **Checkpoint** on pages 61–62. After completing **Checkpoint** and discussing the answers, you can use **Activity #4** (see page 175).

Checkpoint Answers

1. Knowledge about the company, knowledge about the job, and knowledge about what you want.

2. **Company**—What are the products and services; what are the salaries and benefits; how do the employees feel; what are the company's plans for the future? **Job**—Working hours; working conditions; will it be interesting; who will you work with; salary; raises; what skills and strengths will be required; opportunities for promotion; related occupations; does it fit your current ideas and ambitions?

3. Ask yourself why you want this job. For security? To have an income? For a career track? All three? How long would you hope to stay in this job?

4. See page 50 for a complete list of possible questions.

5. Some questions you might ask are the following: What special knowledge, talents, or skills are required for this work? What are the expectations for new hires? What are the most challenging parts of the job? How is an employee evaluated and promoted in this job? What kinds of career opportunities are currently available for my skills, experience, and education?

6. You should not ask the following: How much vacation and sick leave do I get? How long is lunch? How long will I have to work before I get my first raise?

Think On This...

- Have you thought about what it will be like to sit in an interview for a job you really want?

- You know how to dress and some of the questions you might hear, but how will you answer them so that the interviewer feels that you are the best candidate for the job?

- What do you think you could do to make yourself memorable in a positive way?

Chapter Four

During the Interview

CHAPTER OBJECTIVES

1. To learn how to conduct yourself during a job interview.

2. To learn what questions to expect in an interview and how to answer them.

3. To learn how to guide the job interview and sell your accomplishments.

4. To learn what you should do after the interview.

Working Vocabulary

● **Candidate.** A *candidate* is someone who is being considered for a job.

● **Amends.** Whatever is done to make up for a wrong that was committed is called *amends.*

● **Insight.** Having *insight* means being able to give more than the obvious information.

Presentation Suggestions

Begin chapter 4 by discussing **Think On This...** from the end of chapter 3. The students should be able to then come up with three or four objectives for chapter 4 based on **Think On This....** Write their suggestions on the board/overhead. Compare their suggestions to the actual **Chapter Objectives** for chapter 4.

Present the three **Working Vocabulary** words individually and add them to the lists from the previous chapters. Use this opportunity to review all the vocabulary words from chapters 1 through 3.

Ask a student to read aloud "What the Interviewer Wants to Know" on page 64. Ask the class where they have seen this information before. The students should recognize the information from chapter 3.

Ask another student to read aloud "Your Goals in the Interview" at the bottom of page 64. When the reading is finished, ask the students to write the two goals for an interview on the front of their **yellow folders** in bold print.

Read aloud page 65, "Begin the Interview." As you read these tips, write them on the board/overhead in condensed form. For example:

1. Pause.

2. Greet.

3. Sit up straight.

4. Don't smoke or chew gum.

5. Smile.

6. Relax.

7. Let the interviewer start; don't interrupt.

8. Get ready to guide the interview.

Have the students complete **Think About It** on page 66 individually.

Use the following diagram to graphically present the information from pages 67–68 (see page 185 for a transparency master):

GUIDE THE INTERVIEW!		
TALK ABOUT YOURSELF	HOW YOU WOULD BENEFIT THE COMPANY	PRESENT QUALIFICATIONS

The three-column presentation enables you to fill in any relevant information, questions, or answers that the class might want to add as the section is read.

Assign "Guide the Interview" on pages 67–68 to be read silently. When the majority of the class is finished reading, ask for volunteers to put information in the space under the topics of the three-column chart on the board/overhead.

Ask a student to read aloud "Sell Your Accomplishments" and "If You Have Options, Feel Free to Ask Questions" on page 69. Have the students complete **Think About It** on page 70.

Discuss the idea of *flow*. Ask the following question:

- *"What does* flow *mean in this sentence: The* **flow** *of the conversation was interrupted by the telephone ringing."* (Answer: The word *flow* means the rhythm and speed.)

Ask a student to read aloud "The Flow of the Interview" on page 71. Ask the students to describe the flow of a good interview.

Read aloud "Listening and Answering: A Three-Step Process" on page 71. Show the Three-Step Process on the board/overhead, as in the following diagram (see page 186 for a transparency master):

STEP 1: UNDERSTAND WHAT IS REALLY BEING ASKED.	STEP 2: PRESENT THE FACTS TO MAKE YOURSELF LOOK GOOD.	STEP 3: GIVE EXAMPLES TO SUPPORT YOUR BEST SKILLS.

Follow the same pattern as in the preceding diagram by filling in information from the following pages that further clarifies the steps. This information will vary depending on the needs of the class.

Choose four students to read the information on page 72. The first student will read aloud the sample interview question, "How will you get to work if you take this job?" The second student will read the step 1 section, the third student will read the step 2 section, and the fourth student will read the step 3 section. As each section is read, return to the board/overhead display to add to the topic headings as needed.

Continue reading aloud by calling on a student to read "Good Listening Helps You Give Good Answers" on page 73.

The next section on pages 74–80 is all about practicing answering sample interview questions. This will act as the activity for this chapter, because it might take quite a bit of time. Explain to the students that they should read the sample question after each step has been completed. Help the students complete this exercise by reading question 1 aloud and allowing time for them to write down their answers. Reread the question and then proceed to step 2. Allow time for the students to write down their responses. Reread the question. Proceed to step 3. Stop at the end of the page to discuss their responses, and allow several volunteers to share their responses orally. It might be necessary for the class to complete the first two questions in this manner. When the students clearly understand the process for these pages, allow time for them to continue at their own pace.

Have the students complete pages 74–80 individually. Allow as much as one hour for this activity.

Call on a student to read aloud pages 81–82, "The Question of Your Criminal Record" and "Questions About Drugs and Alcohol." These topics will require some discussion among the students. Be prepared to answer any questions. This might be a good time to pair off the students so that they can practice discussing each point on page 81. Have one student act as the interviewer and the other act as the person who is interviewing. Then have the students switch roles. Allow approximately 15 minutes to complete this exercise. Follow with a brief question-and-answer session addressing anything that might have come up during the practice session.

Assign pages 83–85 to be read silently. When the majority of the students have finished reading, ask the following questions:

- *"What is the best response to a question about salary expectations?"* (Answer: "I'm open to negotiating the salary.")

- *"Should you give a concrete answer to questions about returning to school or pursuing further opportunities?"* (Answer: No. Say things like "Possibly," "If my job permits...," or "As long as....")

- *"How should you deal with questions about types of people you prefer to work with?"* (Answer: Say "I really have no problems with people.")

- *"Should you go into detail about possible weaknesses you might have?"* (Answer: No. Think about several small things you might be able to say and put a positive spin on them.)

- *"If you were fired from a previous job, how can you speak positively about it?"* (Answer: Say "They let me go because the job was not a good fit for me at that time.")

Ask a student to read aloud "Illegal Questions" on page 86. Be sure the class knows that any detailed personal information should not be addressed in an interview.

Invite another student volunteer to read aloud "What If You Can't Answer an Interview Question?" on page 86. Explain that the students can ask the interviewer to state the question in another way if it's difficult to understand. Tell the students to always take their time and answer the questions as truthfully and directly as they can. If they do not understand the question the interviewer is asking, they should say so. The interviewer will be more impressed with them if they admit they don't understand than if they try to answer and miss the mark completely.

Complete **Think About It** on pages 87–89 in small groups. Discuss the correct answers as a class.

Call on a student to read aloud "Stay Positive and Confident!" and "Speak with Confidence" on pages 89–90. Then break into small groups to complete the "Speak with Confidence" exercises on pages 90–92. Share responses with the whole class. Write several of the best responses on the board/overhead.

Write the following tips for speaking with confidence on the board/overhead in a condensed form, allowing time for the students to copy the list onto the front of their **yellow folders.**

Tips for Speaking with Confidence:

1. Don't put yourself down.

2. Don't use weak words.

3. Use words that show you have faith in yourself (I am...).

4. Address the interviewer's real concern.

Ask a student to read aloud "Make Positive Statements" on page 93. Proceed immediately with reading "Close the Interview" on page 94. Ask the following question:

- *"What things should you expect to happen at the end of an interview?"* (Answer: The interviewer should say when you can expect to hear from the company. Ask when you can call them back. Ask for a business card. If you need to, ask for a day or two to think about any job offer. Thank the interviewer for his or her time.)

Give each student a notebook labeled INTERVIEW JOURNAL. Then call on a student to read aloud "An Interview Journal" on pages 95–96. Tell the students to write each of the bullet point questions on the first page of the journal. Explain that the next time they will use this journal will be after their first real interview. Have them put their journals in their **yellow folders** if possible.

The subject of thank-you notes has been discussed before this chapter. Students will know when they are necessary. The section on page 97 gives more details about what to say in a thank-you note. Ask a student to read this page aloud. Have the students pull out this page and put it in their **yellow folders.**

Call on a student to read aloud both "Follow-Up Calls" and "Keep It Up!" on page 99. Discuss briefly as a class.

Have the students complete **Checkpoint** on page 100 individually. Then discuss the answers with the class.

Checkpoint Answers

1. Accept the job or ask if you can have a day or two to think about it.

2. Each person you talked to during an interview.

3. If more than two weeks have passed since an interview and you haven't heard back from the employer.

4. Who you are; that you interviewed for the _____ position and were wondering if the position had been filled or if they'd made a decision.

5. Fill in your interview journal.

Quick Quiz

Name: _____

Directions: *Complete the following crossword puzzle. The answers are vocabulary words from chapters 3 and 4.*

Across

1. Job

3. Meet with employer to see if they will hire you

4. Person applying for a job

7. Getting more money or responsibility

8. Official paper

Down

2. Getting ahead

5. Repayment, reconciliation

6. Knowing more than the obvious

Quick Quiz Answer Key

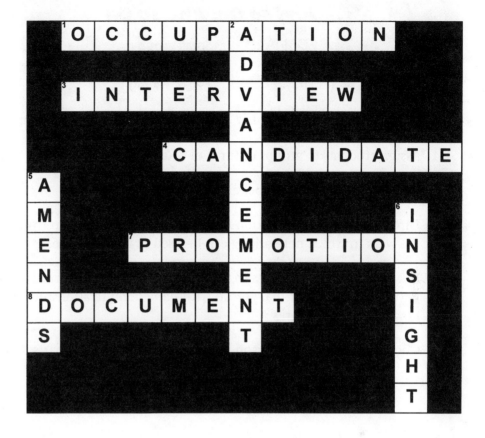

Activity #1

And So On, And So On

FORMAT: Small group

TIME: 10–15 minutes

MATERIALS: The diagram on page 181, chart paper, markers

1. Assign students to groups of three or four.

2. Give each group chart paper and markers.

3. Direct the students' attention to the display of the diagram from page 181. Discuss the ways in which networking can be used in everyday life.

4. Ask each group of students to think of an imaginary person. Then create a networking chart for that person with names and relationships to demonstrate how the network works.

5. Choose a group spokesperson to present the completed charts to the entire class.

Activity #2

Conversational Exchanges

FORMAT: Paired

TIME: 20–25 minutes

MATERIALS: Index cards, paper, pens/pencils, a phone to use
              as a prop

1. Print the words EFFECTIVE and NOT EFFECTIVE on an equal number of index
   cards so that there are enough for one card per pair of students. Some will get the
   EFFECTIVE card and some the NOT EFFECTIVE card.

2. Explain that the paired students are to write and role-play a cold-calling script that
   either works and results in an interview or doesn't and is stopped by a screener.

3. Present the scenes for the entire class and have fun!

Activity #3

Role-Play It

FORMAT: Paired

TIME: 20–30 minutes

MATERIALS: Workbook pages 50–53, paper, pens/pencils

1. Assign a partner to each student.

2. Explain that each pair will be responsible for preparing a two-minute skit demonstrating an interview situation.

3. One student will play the part of the interviewer, and the other will play the part of the job seeker.

4. Students must use the questions and guidelines suggested in the textbook.

5. The skits will be performed for the entire class.

6. After the performances, allow the class to vote for first, second, and third place.

Activity #4

Prepare Taylor

FORMAT: Small group

TIME: 15–20 minutes

MATERIALS: Chart paper, markers, tape, textbook pages 55–60

1. Divide the class into small groups.

2. Have each group choose a person from the group to trace on the chart paper. Have the student lie on the chart paper while another student traces his or her body outline.

3. Use the outline to create "Taylor." (Taylor can be either male or female.)

4. The students will draw the correct type of clothing on the outline and draw anything that "Taylor" will need to be successful at an interview. Remind the students to refer to pages 55–60 for lists of all the things that they should bring to an interview.

5. When the groups have finished, allow time for a group representative to hang and present their well-prepared "Taylor" to the class.

Comprehensive Vocabulary Quiz for Book 4

NETWORKING AND INTERVIEWING FOR JOBS

Directions: *Choose the correct vocabulary word from the four choices. Circle it. Then find the word in the puzzle.*

1. The job of the _____ is to protect the manager's time and privacy.

   network   screener
   occupation   candidate

2. Available jobs are often referred to as the _____ .

   insight   referral
   job market   script

3. Moving up in the company through promotions is a type of _____ .

   promotion   potential
   advancement   amends

4. A(n) _____ for a job is the person who is interviewing.

   potential   candidate
   referral   organization

5. Bring _____ , or official papers, to an interview.

   documents   network
   leads   insight

6. Calling someone you don't know is _____ .

   script   cold-calling
   occupation   screener

7. People make _____ to try to right a wrong.

    insight   potential
    referral   amends

8. If you work very well, an employer might give you a(n) _____ .

    organization   network
    potential   promotion

9. Someone who is working for a company you are interested in might be able
    to give you a(n) _____ .

    interview   script
    referral   occupation

10. After you know what job a company has to offer, you have gained some
    _____ into what kind of person they want to hire.

    referral   insight
    leads   potential

11. A face-to-face meeting to discuss a job opening is a(n) _____ .

    occupation   script
    promotion   interview

12. A(n) _____ is a written conversation that tells you what to say.

    candidate   script
    insight   screener

13. _____ are suggestions generated by people about job openings they
    know about.

    advancement   leads
    occupation   job market

14. The ability to possibly do something good or bad is _____ .

    promotion   insight
    potential   document

15. _____ is another word for a job or career.

    interview   occupation
    organization   referral

16. The people you know and the people they know are your _____ .

    interview   insight
    job market   network

17. A company or service _____ is a good place to look for volunteer opportunities that might lead to full-time paid employment.

    leads   organization
    occupation   job market

C	N	O	I	T	A	P	U	C	C	O	F	I	G	M
R	O	X	L	Y	W	E	I	V	R	E	T	N	I	O
J	I	L	L	A	I	T	N	E	T	O	P	S	G	N
D	T	J	D	K	R	L	E	A	D	S	I	I	C	E
W	A	N	T	C	A	R	D	V	H	X	R	G	E	T
G	Z	F	E	J	A	I	E	C	D	F	C	H	S	W
O	I	P	K	M	D	L	Y	F	E	D	S	T	D	O
F	N	O	R	N	E	Z	L	G	E	Z	M	F	N	R
K	A	J	A	O	C	C	T	I	B	R	K	I	E	K
N	G	C	M	U	M	H	N	C	N	V	G	N	M	Z
E	R	A	B	N	A	O	C	A	C	G	E	W	A	A
I	O	S	O	O	T	X	T	I	V	E	W	X	Y	K
M	W	D	J	X	D	N	C	I	R	D	Z	I	V	R
J	L	B	T	N	E	M	U	C	O	D	A	I	O	F
A	R	G	G	U	U	T	S	S	C	N	C	O	D	Z

Answer Key

1. screener
2. job market
3. advancement
4. candidate
5. documents
6. cold-calling
7. amends
8. promotion
9. referral
10. insight
11. interview
12. script
13. leads
14. potential
15. occupation
16. network
17. organization

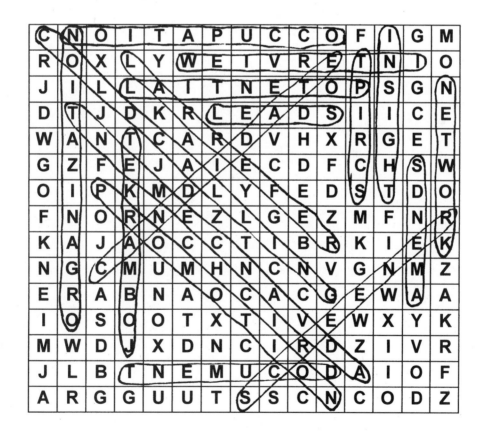

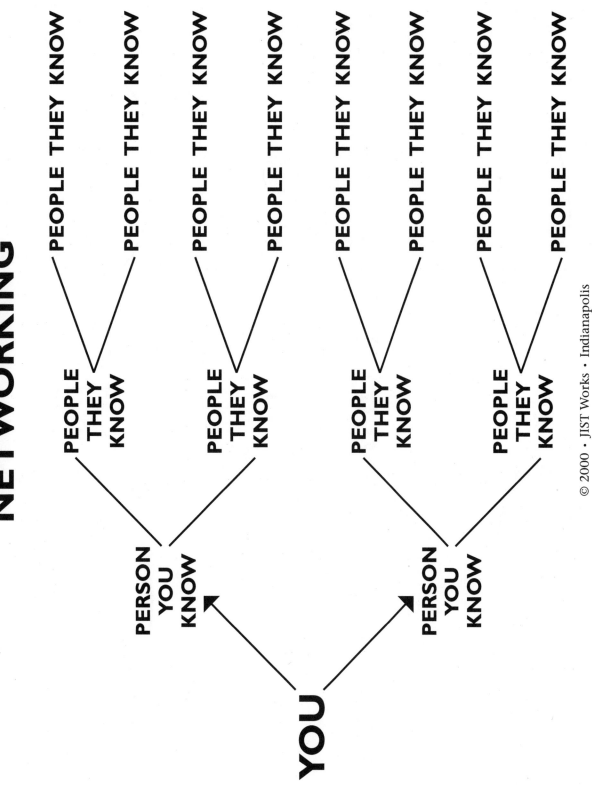

NETWORKING

PEOPLE THEY KNOW

PEOPLE THEY KNOW

PEOPLE THEY KNOW

PEOPLE THEY KNOW

PEOPLE THEY KNOW

PEOPLE THEY KNOW

PEOPLE THEY KNOW

PEOPLE THEY KNOW

PEOPLE THEY KNOW

PEOPLE THEY KNOW

PEOPLE THEY KNOW

PEOPLE THEY KNOW

PERSON YOU KNOW

PERSON YOU KNOW

YOU

© 2000 • JIST Works • Indianapolis

From chapter 1, page 145

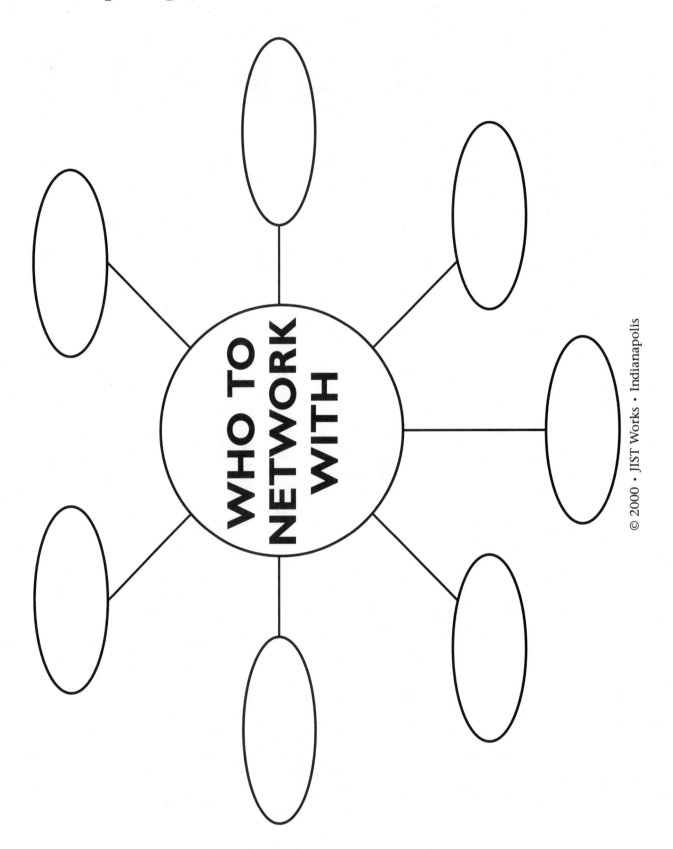

WHO TO NETWORK WITH

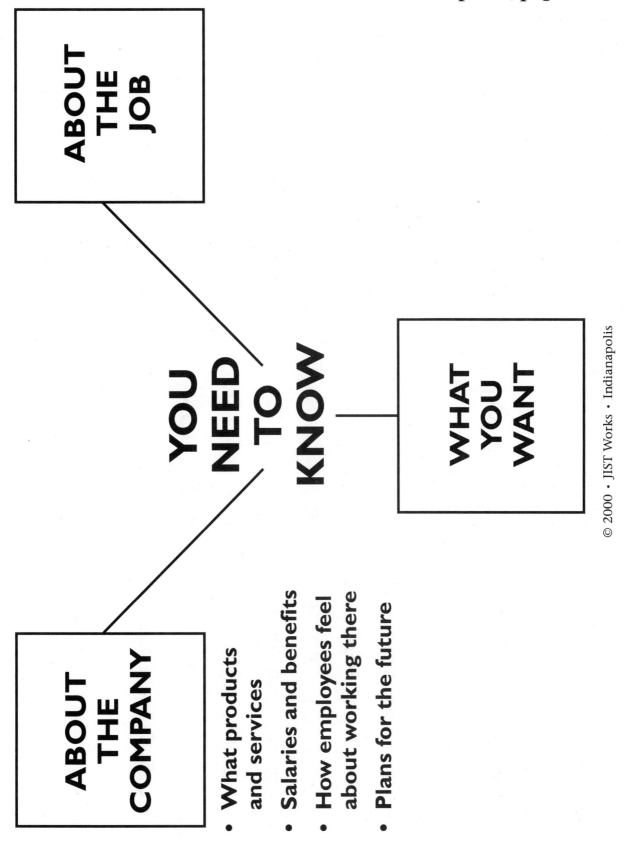

ABOUT THE JOB

YOU NEED TO KNOW

WHAT YOU WANT

ABOUT THE COMPANY

- What products and services
- Salaries and benefits
- How employees feel about working there
- Plans for the future

From chapter 3, page 161

BRING THESE TO AN INTERVIEW!

* RESUME

* DRIVER'S LICENSE

* MILITARY RECORDS

* SCHOOL CERTIFICATES

* BIRTH CERTIFICATE

* SOCIAL SECURITY CARD

* LETTERS OF RECOMMENDATION

* U.S. COAST GUARD MERCHANT MARINER CARD

* UNION CARD

* DIPLOMA

* SCHOOL ID CARD

* NOTEPAD

* PEN

From chapter 4, page 165

GUIDE THE INTERVIEW!

TALK ABOUT YOURSELF	HOW YOU WOULD BENEFIT THE COMPANY	PRESENT QUALIFICATIONS

© 2000 • JIST Works • Indianapolis

STEP 1: UNDERSTAND WHAT IS REALLY BEING ASKED.	STEP 2: PRESENT THE FACTS TO MAKE YOURSELF LOOK GOOD.	STEP 3: GIVE EXAMPLES TO SUPPORT YOUR BEST SKILLS.

PART V

Instructor's Resources for

KEEPING YOUR JOB:

SURVIVE AND SUCCEED IN A NEW JOB

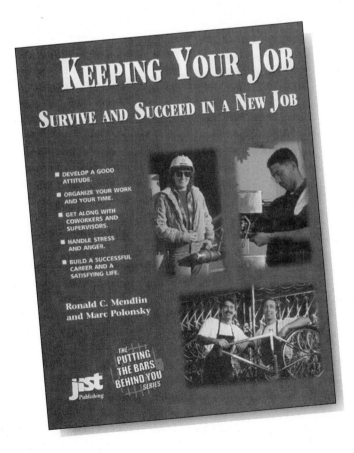

KEEPING YOUR JOB

SURVIVE AND SUCCEED IN A NEW JOB

■ DEVELOP A GOOD ATTITUDE.

■ ORGANIZE YOUR WORK AND YOUR TIME.

■ GET ALONG WITH COWORKERS AND SUPERVISORS.

■ HANDLE STRESS AND ANGER.

■ BUILD A SUCCESSFUL CAREER AND A SATISFYING LIFE.

Ronald C. Mendlin and Marc Polonsky

THE PUTTING THE BARS BEHIND YOU SERIES

jist Publishing

Workbook Table of Contents

Keeping Your Job: Survive and Succeed in a New Job

Chapter One

The Basics

CHAPTER OBJECTIVES

1. To learn the basic principles of being a good employee.

2. To learn what it means to have a good attitude at work.

3. To learn how to do the best job possible and fit in well at work.

Working Vocabulary

- **Attitude.** An *attitude* is the image and feelings you project toward a person, place, thing, or idea.

- **Supervisor.** A *supervisor* may also be known as a boss. Your supervisor is the person who hires you, makes sure you know how to do your job, gives you raises, and can fire you.

- **Efficient.** Wasting no time and doing a good job requires an employee to be *efficient*.

- **Honesty.** Speaking the truth and doing the right thing shows *honesty*.

- **Respect.** Taking the time to think and consider other people's views and ideas, even if you don't share them, is showing *respect*.

- **Flexible.** Being *flexible* is the ability to change work schedules and duties without undue disruption.

- **Harassment.** Persistent disturbing and irritating behavior is *harassment*.

Presentation Suggestions

Begin the class by writing the **Chapter Objectives** on the board/overhead. Read each one aloud and discuss with the class why each is necessary in the workplace. Start a discussion about what the students already know about the workplace, either good or bad experiences.

Next, introduce the **Working Vocabulary** words. Read each word and definition one at a time, making sure that the students can relate the word to their own life. Post these on the board/overhead or chart paper and keep them displayed in the room. Add each chapter's **Working Vocabulary** list to this one as the students progress through the workbook.

Call on a student to read aloud "Be on Time Every Day" and "Personal Grooming and Appearance" on page 4. Ask the following questions:

- *"Give two reasons why it's important to be on time every day for your new job."* (Answers: The employer depends on you; you made a commitment; tardiness causes stress for everyone; you will lose your job if you are not on time every day.)

- *"What should you do if you have to miss a day's work?"* (Answer: If possible, let your employer know as far in advance as you can.)

- *"Explain what is meant by an unofficial dress code."* (Answer: A style of dress that is not spelled out in written form but is obviously expected, judging by what the other workers are wearing.)

After answering these questions, ask another student to read aloud "Come to the Job Fit and Alert" on pages 4 and 5. Ask the following question:

- *"Name at least three ways you can be sure to be at your best when you are at work."* (Answers: Don't stay out late at night; eat breakfast; leave home on a good note; think ahead to avoid as many problems as possible.)

Ask a student volunteer to read the part of George in the **Example** on page 5. Pull out these words from the paragraph and write them on the board/overhead:

Early	Positively
Focused	Challenges
Conditioned	

Ask the students to think of a sentence about work that uses all of these words. Write several of their examples on the board/overhead. If the students have difficulty getting started, give them this example:

Get up **early** to **focus** your mind and be **conditioned** to face the **challenges** of the day **positively.**

The words do not have to remain in the same order, but the meanings of the words must stay the same.

Complete **Think About It** on pages 5–6.

Give each student a sheet of lined paper. Call on a student to read aloud "Know Your Work and Do It Well" on page 7. Ask the student to read the section line by line, stopping after each bullet point. Ask the class to restate each statement in their own words. Write the reworded statements on the board/overhead. Some of these will be easier than others due to their short length. Emphasize to the students that the idea behind this exercise is to state the basic idea in a short form. The students will write the reworded statements on their lined paper.

Give each student a **purple folder.** Ask the students to place the paper in their folders. Have the students write their names on the front of their folders and maybe one of the goals from pages 5 and 6 under their names.

Invite a student to read aloud "Take Notes" on page 8. After the student has finished reading, ask the following questions:

- *"What is the best thing to use to take notes?"* (Answer: Index cards or small notepads.)

- *"If you decide to take notes, what should you do with them?"* (Answer: Read them over from time to time to remind yourself of the important points of the job and to remember how far you have come.)

- *"What does taking notes show your supervisors?"* (Answer: That you are serious about learning to do your job well.)

Ask a student to read aloud "Keep a Positive Attitude" on page 9. Review the definition of *attitude* as it appeared in the **Working Vocabulary** section. Have another student read the part of Bill and someone else read the part of George in the **Examples** on page 9. After the student completes reading the part of Bill, ask the class to put into their own words what he meant by "it's gonna spread to all areas of his life." Next, have the other student read the part of George. Ask the following question:

- *"What might happen if George's mind wandered to the disappointing and frustrating areas of his life?"* (Answer: Answers will vary.)

Point out the words *honesty* and *respect* in the **Working Vocabulary** list. Review the definitions orally and ask the students to guess how each of these words affects the workplace. Write these ideas on the board/overhead.

Then ask a student to read aloud "Honesty and Respect" on page 10. Refer to the ideas on the board. Ask the students to add something or change anything that they feel is incorrect. Give each student an index card and allow time for them to copy these ideas. Have the students place these cards in their **purple folders.**

Choose a student to read aloud "Be Flexible" on page 11. After the student is done reading, go back to the definition of *flexible* from the **Working Vocabulary** section. Ask the following questions:

- *"After reading this section, what do think an undue disruption might be?"* (Answer: Undue disruptions are anger, rage, or physical violence.)

- *"What is the best way to remain flexible in a difficult situation that might require more adjustment than you thought?"* (Answer: Use your creative thinking to remain flexible even in difficult situations.)

Choose a volunteer to read the part of Bill in the **Example** on page 12. Have the students complete **Think About It** on page 12 individually. Allow time for them to share their responses orally if they want to.

Ask a student to read aloud "Workplace Rules" and "Sexual Harassment" on pages 13 and 14. Use this section to discuss and answer any questions the students might have about sexual harassment in the workplace. Allow plenty of time, because this is a difficult concept for some people to grasp, yet it is very important. It might be helpful to have a pamphlet about sexual harassment for each of the students, as well as a book about employment law. You can get these by calling the local library or local government offices. Many prison libraries might also have books on employment law in their collections.

Choose someone to read aloud "Unwritten Rules" on page 14. Then ask a volunteer to read Bill's part in the **Example** at the bottom of page 14. Follow with **Activity #1** (see page 225). Complete **Think About It** on page 15 in small groups. Share these responses as a class.

Ask a student to read aloud page 16, "Using Computers." Many of the students may never have had a chance to see or work with a computer, so you might need to explain what computers are and what they help people do. Continue by inviting another student to read aloud "Use Your Head" on page 17. Ask the following question:

- *"What things can you do to make sure you are using your head?"* (Answers: Don't just get by; use common sense; think before you speak or act; be respectful; don't act impulsively.)

Choose another student to read Reggie's part in the **Example** at the bottom of page 17. Move on immediately to complete **Checkpoint** on page 18. When the students have finished, review the correct answers as a class.

Checkpoint Answers

1. If there is a dress code, follow it. If there is no dress code, dress in clean, conservative clothing.

2. You should go to work with a positive attitude.

3. To learn your work well, take notes and try to pick up on any unwritten rules in the workplace.

4. Knowing how to work on a computer is important because almost all offices and businesses today rely on computers for day-to-day business.

5. Think before you act when you are on the job. Think ahead to anticipate what the consequences of your actions might be.

Think On This...

● Once you have a job, how much time will it take?

● Are you willing to work a nontraditional schedule that might include nights and weekends?

● If you have to restructure your schedule, how will you manage your time?

● If you learn to manage your time better, do you think it will have a positive effect on other parts of your life?

● If so, which parts?

Chapter Two

Organize Your Work

CHAPTER OBJECTIVES

1. To learn basic principles for organizing your work.

2. To manage your time well.

3. To keep a positive attitude for managing your work and your time.

Working Vocabulary

● **Organized.** Being *organized* means having control, making plans, and following patterns.

● **Quota.** The amount of work that is supposed to be completed in a certain amount of time is a *quota*.

● **Prioritizing.** *Prioritizing* means putting things in order based on what should be done first.

Presentation Suggestions

Begin the session by discussing the **Think On This...** from chapter 1. Write these points on the board/overhead. Then write the **Chapter Objectives** on the board/overhead. Allow time for the students to read each of the posted writings silently. Then ask the students to state any similarities between the two. Write these on the board/overhead.

Introduce the three **Working Vocabulary** words one at a time. Post these words and definitions in the room, adding them to the **Working Vocabulary** from chapter 1.

Focus the class on the word *organization*. Ask the students to give examples of people they think are organized and why they think they are. Ask them to give examples of what makes these people organized. Then call on a student to read aloud "Why Is Organization Important?" on page 20. Ask the following question:

● *"What is the first thing you can do when you begin a new job and are learning about it?"* (Answer: Make a plan.)

Call on another student to read "Tips for Effective Organization" on pages 20 and 21. As the student reads aloud, ask him to stop briefly after each bullet point so that the class can discuss the point. Write each topic sentence (the sentence in bold print) on the board/overhead and then discuss it. When the student has finished reading, allow time for the students to copy the bullet point list onto the front of their **purple folders.** Ask the following questions:

● *"What is likely to happen if you have a concrete goal in mind?"* (Answer: You will be more productive.)

● *"Describe a well-organized desk."* (Answer: Very little clutter; papers in stacks of related materials; use of files; desktop is clear.)

- *"What does the statement 'Nothing is particularly hard if you divide it into small parts' mean?"* (Answer: If you break down a difficult task into smaller parts and tackle the small parts one at a time, the task will be easier to manage.)

Call on a student volunteer to read the part of Jill in the **Example** on page 21. After the section is read, allow time for the class to discuss the steps involved in seismic retrofitting. Write the steps on the board/overhead. The students will have to guess at some of the steps, but they will get the idea of breaking down a job into smaller parts. (*Hint:* Seismic retrofitting has to do with preparing older homes for earthquakes.)

Write the words MANAGE YOUR TIME on the board/overhead. Direct the students' attention to the first bullet point on page 22. They should recognize it as one of the **Working Vocabulary** words. Review the definition of *prioritize*.

Then call on a student to read aloud page 22 and the top of page 23. Proceed in the same manner as you did on pages 20 and 21: Have the student read each bullet point paragraph, stopping briefly after each to allow for a bit of discussion. Write the bullet points under the heading on the board/overhead. When the student is finished reading, have the students copy the bullet point list onto the front of their **purple folders**, next to the list for organization.

Ask the students the following questions:

- *"What does* prioritize *mean?"* (Answer: To put things in order of their importance.)

- *"Why is it important to follow through with a plan you begin?"* (Answer: You will reach your goals faster.)

- *"Describe the argument in favor of a light lunch."* (Answer: A heavy lunch might make you sluggish in the afternoon hours; a light lunch will give you needed energy without slowing you down.)

Ask a student to read the part of George in the **Example** on page 23. Then discuss it with the class. Follow with **Activity #2** (see page 226). Share these responses on a volunteer basis. Then complete **Think About It** on pages 24–25. Discuss the answers as a group.

Choose a student to read aloud page 25, "How Your Attitude Affects Time Management and Organization." Follow the same steps as before when the student is reading. Create a bullet point list on the board/overhead under the heading EFFECTS OF ATTITUDE. When the student has finished reading, allow time for the students to copy the list onto the back of their **purple folders.**

Ask the following questions:

- *"What is the big picture?"* (Answer: Remembering who you are, where you came from, and where you are going.)

- *"Give some examples of positive thoughts that could help you through the day."* (Answer: Answers will vary.)

Have a student read the part of George in the **Example** on page 26.

Complete **Think About It** on pages 26–27 in small groups. Share responses as a class.

Complete **Checkpoint** on page 28. When the students have completed the **Checkpoint** exercise, review the correct responses with them.

Checkpoint Answers

1. Set goals; break down big tasks into smaller tasks; put tasks in order of urgency; cut problems into smaller parts and attack the smaller parts first.

2. Prioritize; Set small and large goals; follow through; do related or similar activities at about the same time; eat a light lunch; don't be ruled by the telephone; look for ways to save time on tasks.

3. Don't be too hard on yourself; look forward, not back; do an honest day's work; keep the big picture in mind.

Quick Quiz

Name: _____

Directions: *Complete the following crossword puzzle. The answers are vocabulary words from chapters 1 and 2.*

Across

1. Boss

3. Quick and correct

6. Unwanted attention

8. Adaptable

9. Required amount

10. Neat and in order

Down

2. Putting in order of importance

4. How you feel about something

5. Truthfulness

7. Consideration for

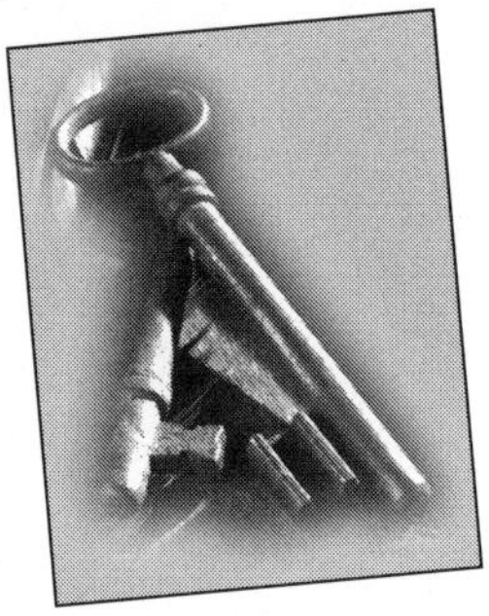

Quick Quiz Answer Key

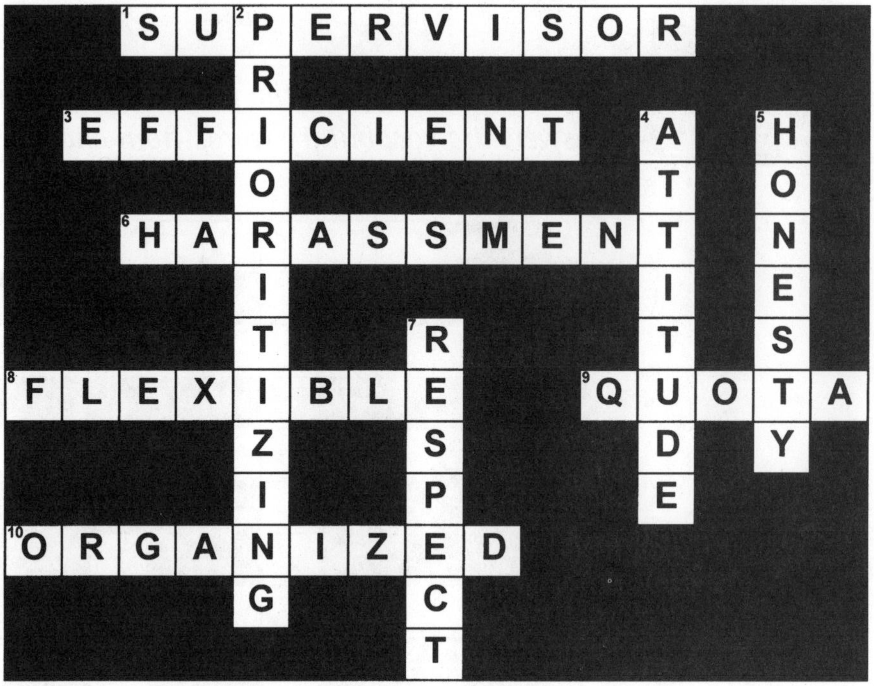
1 SUPERVISOR
2 PRIORITIZING
3 EFFICIENT
4 ATTITUDE
5 HONESTY
6 HARASSMENT
7 RESPECT
8 FLEXIBLE
9 QUOTA
10 ORGANIZED

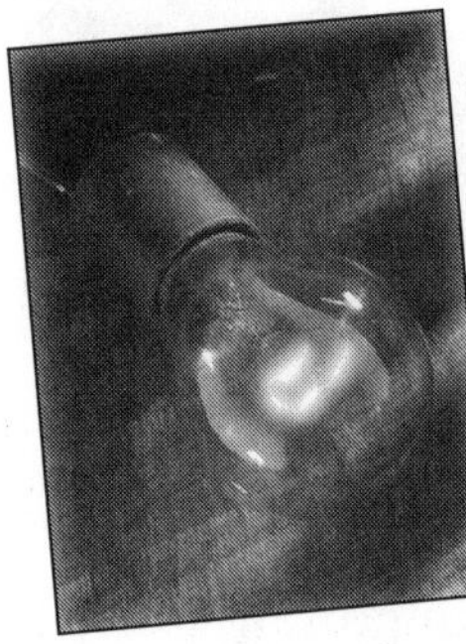

Think On This...

So, how are your stress-management skills? Surely you don't think you can find a stress-free job, do you? That job hasn't been found yet, by anyone. Often the stress at work depends on the people you have to work with.

- When a sticky situation happens at work, how are you equipped to handle it?
- Are there any ways you can think of to get along with coworkers, handle problems, and earn the respect of your coworkers and supervisors?

Chapter Three

Get Along with Coworkers and Supervisors

CHAPTER OBJECTIVES

1. To get along well with people at work.

2. To handle conflict situations that might come up at work.

3. To get along well with supervisors and coworkers while earning their respect.

Working Vocabulary

- **Constructive comments.** Use *constructive comments* to compliment people sincerely when they do something well.

- **Gossip.** Saying bad things about other people without their knowledge is *gossip.*

- **Manners.** The use of proper behavior, including courtesy and politeness, is all a part of *manners.*

- **Diplomatic.** Being polite and using caution when dealing with other people is being *diplomatic.*

- **Negotiate.** Discussing and conferring with others in order to reach a mutually agreeable decision means to *negotiate.*

- **Dependability.** The degree to which someone can be trusted is his or her *dependability.*

- **Mentor.** A *mentor* is someone older and more experienced that you can learn from.

Presentation Suggestions

Begin the class by discussing the **Think On This...** assignment from the end of chapter 2. Allow ample time for the students to share experiences, both positive and negative, that they have had with coworkers in the past. Using this discussion, ask the students to come up with at least three goals they think will be outlined in chapter 3. Write their suggestions on the board/overhead.

Then present the actual **Chapter Objectives.** Write these in a column next to the suggested goals. Have the students point out the similarities and differences between their suggested goals and the chapter's actual goals. If their goals are different enough that there are very few similarities, you may do one of two things:

- Add their goals to the actual list.

- Return to the **Think On This...** section and ask the students to explain where they got the ideas for their suggested goals. This option requires the students to justify their earlier responses.

Present the **Working Vocabulary** words for chapter 3. Read through the list, presenting each word and definition individually. Then go back through the complete list of **Working Vocabulary** words and review all the words and definitions. Add the words and definitions from chapter 3 to the posted list.

Call on a student to read "Why Is Getting Along with Coworkers and Supervisors Important?", "Know Their Names," and the **Example**, all on page 30. When the student has finished reading, ask the following questions:

- *"Why do you think that success depends 85 percent on personality and only 15 percent on training? Wouldn't you think it would be the other way around?"* (Answer: Answers will vary. Discuss that this means that their attitudes toward their jobs and the people they work with are even more important to job satisfaction than having previous training.)

- *"Explain how you feel if someone you have known for a while never seems to remember your name. Do you think people you work with might feel the same?"* (Answer: Answers will vary.)

- *"What is George's trick for remembering people's names?"* (Answer: Using rhyming catch phrases that remind you of the person.)

Ask a student to read aloud "Cheerfulness" on page 31. Discuss the difference between being cheerful and being phony. Talk about some ways the students can try to remain cheerful, even when they might not feel like it. Write their suggestions, if appropriate, on the board/overhead. Then give each student an index card so that they can copy the three suggestions they think will work best for them. Have the students put the cards in their **purple folders.**

Choose a student to read "More Tips for Getting Along with Others at Work" on pages 31–32. Instruct the student to read each bullet point and then then stop briefly so that you can write the bullet point on the board/overhead, discuss it, and then have the students copy the bullet point onto the back of their **purple folders.** Proceed in this manner until the class has read and discussed each bullet point on pages 31 and 32.

Break the class into groups of three or four. Give each group two sheets of chart paper and markers. Explain to the groups that they will be drawing two pictures. The pictures will show two types of workers: one they want to work with and one they don't want to work with. Allow 10–15 minutes for the students to draw their examples. Ask a student from each group to present their examples to the entire class. If space is available, display their drawings in the classroom. Call on a student to read aloud "The Kind of Person You *Don't* Want to Be" and "The Kind of Person You *Do* Want to Be" on page 33. Ask the following question:

- *"Do you all think your drawings reflect the things that are mentioned on page 33?"* (Answer: Answers will vary.)

Ask a volunteer to read the part of George in the **Example** on page 33. Allow time for the students to discuss and share their experiences in small groups. Complete **Think About It** on page 34.

Ask another student to read aloud page 35, "Deal with Conflict at Work." Use the following diagram to begin the presentation of page 35 (see page 233 for a transparency master):

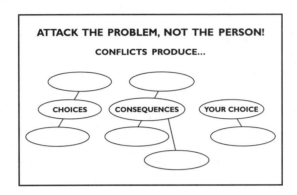

Direct the students' attention to the sentence at the top of the board/overhead: ATTACK THE PROBLEM, NOT THE PERSON! Ask the students to explain in their own words what they think this sentence means. Then direct their attention to the words CONFLICTS, CHOICES, CONSEQUENCES, and YOUR CHOICE. Ask the students to come up with a conflict that might happen at work. Write this in the space next to the word CONFLICTS. Next, ask the students to provide several choices about what to do to solve this conflict. Write these connecting to the word CHOICES. Now ask the students to provide what they believe will be some of the consequences of the choices they picked. Write these on the board/overhead, attached to the word CONSEQUENCES. Last, ask the class to decide on the final choice that would give the best results and the best consequences. Write this on the board/overhead attached to the words YOUR CHOICE. This exercise must be done at least three times with three separate conflicts in order for the students to begin to understand the process of solving conflicts at work.

Follow with **Activity #3** (see page 227).

Choose two different students to read aloud the parts of Sammy and George in the **Examples** on page 36. When they have finished reading, ask the class, "Would someone share with us a way you cool off after a disagreement or a way you have seen someone else cool off—a way that works without causing a scene?" (Answer: Answers will vary.)

Have the students complete **Think About It** on pages 36–37 individually, and then assign small groups to discuss the responses.

Choose a student to read aloud "Supervisors" on page 38. When the reading is finished, ask the following questions:

- *"What should you show your supervisor from day one?"* (Answer: That you are cooperative and responsible.)

- *"If you show that you are these things, what will the supervisor do for you in return?"* (Answer: Your supervisor will trust you.)

- *"Should you expect your supervisor to give you instructions and respectful criticisms?"* (Answer: Yes.)

- *"How should you respond to these criticisms?"* (Answer: With a respectful attitude and the willingness to do what is asked.)

Ask a student volunteer to read aloud the part of Sammy in the **Example** at the bottom of page 38. When the student has finished, discuss this short paragraph briefly. Move on to "Tips for Getting Along Well with Supervisors" on page 39. Choose another student to read this section aloud. If the preceding diagram was left up on the board/ overhead, use it to begin a discussion about conflicts with supervisors. If not, redraw the diagram or put it back up and use it again to guide the students through the Three-Step Process.

Choose two student volunteers to read the parts of Bill and Susan in the **Examples** on page 40. Ask the following question:

- *"Do these reactions seem similar to the reactions we thought of in our discussions about conflicts and consequences?"* (Answer: Yes.)

Ask a student to read aloud "What Your Employer Looks For" on pages 40–41. Write the bullet points on the board/overhead where students can easily read and refer to them. The following diagram is an example of how this should look (see page 234 for a transparency master):

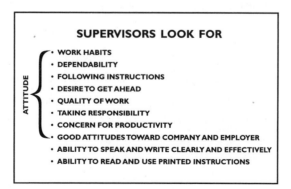

SUPERVISORS LOOK FOR

ATTITUDE {
- WORK HABITS
- DEPENDABILITY
- FOLLOWING INSTRUCTIONS
- DESIRE TO GET AHEAD
- QUALITY OF WORK
- TAKING RESPONSIBILITY
- CONCERN FOR PRODUCTIVITY
- GOOD ATTITUDES TOWARD COMPANY AND EMPLOYER
- ABILITY TO SPEAK AND WRITE CLEARLY AND EFFECTIVELY
- ABILITY TO READ AND USE PRINTED INSTRUCTIONS

Point out any of these that appear to be related in any way. Ask the students which of these points they feel they have already accomplished and which points they feel they have to work on the most. Give each student a sheet of lined paper to copy this list, as well as any notes that the class feels are appropriate, and have them put it in their **purple folders.**

Choose someone to read aloud the part of George in the **Example** on page 41. Then briefly discuss this section with the class.

Call on a student to read aloud page 42, "Make Suggestions." When the student has finished, ask the following questions:

- *"Why is it a good idea to try to make some suggestions to your employer?"* (Answer: To win the employer's respect.)

- *"What do you think a good suggestion tells an employer about you?"* (Answers: That you are using your head at work; that you are noticing what things could be improved for the good of the company; that you are a self starter.)

Choose someone to read the part of Reggie in the **Example** at the bottom of page 42. Discuss.

Write the word MENTOR on the board/overhead. Ask a student to refer to the **Working Vocabulary** words for the definition of the word. Ask the class if anyone has ever had a mentor before, perhaps in school or at a previous job. Discuss. Then, as a class, look at "Mentors" and "Why It's Good to Have a Mentor" on page 43. Ask the students to come up with ways a mentor could help them with each of these points.

Pick a student to read "Choose a Mentor" on page 43 and "More Than One Mentor" on page 44. Ask the students to write the name of at least one person they feel meets the qualifications of a mentor on their **purple folders.** This person should be someone they feel they could lean on a bit for guidance when they are released from prison. Suggest former teachers, coaches, and ministers.

Assign the section "Develop a Mentor Relationship" to be read silently. Then ask the following question:

- *"Will all mentoring relationships work out well?"* (Answer: Not all, but you have to begin slowly to develop a good working relationship.)

Read aloud "Self-Mentoring" at the bottom of page 44. Then ask a student volunteer to read aloud "How Your Coworkers See You" on page 45. When they have finished reading this section, ask the question on the following page.

- *"Even if you are the type of person who doesn't really care what other people think of you, how can it benefit you to think about how you are perceived by other workers?"* (Answer: If your coworkers like you, they will be more likely to put in a good word for you; they might be more willing to help you, and the workload will be a little easier; you will be happier at your job and feel more successful.)

Complete **Think About It** on page 46 in small groups and discuss the responses as a class.

Then have the students complete **Checkpoint** on pages 47 and 48 individually. Discuss the answers with the class.

Checkpoint Answers

1. Compromise; think before you act, and then act calmly; discuss the problem with a supervisor; go for a short walk; take a 10-minute break to get away from the problem.

2. Any of the following: work habits; dependability; following instructions; desire to get ahead; quality of work; taking responsibility; concern for productivity; good attitudes toward the company and employer; ability to speak and write clearly and effectively; ability to read and use printed instructions.

3. Any of the following: how cooperative you are; how helpful you are to other coworkers; whether or not you compete with other coworkers to look good in front of the supervisor; how easy you are to get along with; how cheerful you are; how organized you are; how dependable and hardworking you are.

4. A mentor can help you do the following: understand your work; take on new challenges at work; keep up your energy, spirit, and enthusiasm; increase your confidence and skills; avoid unnecessary mistakes; qualify for promotions; achieve your goals at work.

5. You can benefit from more than one person's knowledge.

6. Someone you respect, whom you feel is knowledgeable, and who does his or her job with integrity; someone who is thoughtful and kind and willing to help you.

7. By learning from people you admire; encouraging yourself; reading, listening, and watching; associating yourself with productive and inspiring people; holding yourself responsible.

Quick Quiz

Name: _____

Directions: *Complete the following crossword puzzle.*
The answers are vocabulary words from chapter 3.

Across

2. Polite and tactful

4. Mutual agreement

5. Polite behavior

6. Spread rumors

7. Useful and helpful

Down

1. Being counted on

3. Someone who guides

Quick Quiz Answer Key

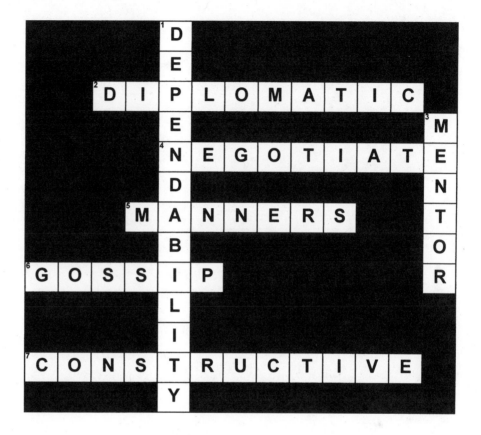

Crossword puzzle answers:

1. DEPENDABILITY (down)
2. DIPLOMATIC (across)
3. MENTOR (down)
4. NEGOTIATE (across)
5. MANNERS (across)
6. GOSSIP (across)
7. CONSTRUCTIVE (across)

Think On This...

Sometimes dealing with conflicts at work might cause you to feel stressed.

● What are some ways that you deal with stress?

● Have you ever felt so stressed that you have given up?

● Why should you try to avoid that feeling?

Chapter Four

Handle Stress at Work

CHAPTER OBJECTIVES

1. To learn what stress is and what it does to people.

2. To learn ways of relieving and avoiding stress.

3. To learn ways to handle the anger that comes from stress.

4. To learn physical exercises for releasing stress.

5. To learn what burnout is and how to handle it.

Working Vocabulary

- **Stress.** The feeling of anxiety, tension, and pressure in certain situations is known as *stress*.

- **Micromanagement.** *Micromanagement* is too much supervision of the smallest details.

- **Relapse.** Going back to drinking or using drugs is a *relapse*.

- **Relieving.** Getting rid of something that is bothersome is an act of *relieving*.

- **Meditation.** Quiet thinking time that is used to focus the mind and relax the body is *meditation*.

- **Anxiety.** An extreme form of stress that causes racing pulse, sweating, dizziness, and shortness of breath is *anxiety*.

Presentation Suggestions

Note: Due to the number of group activities included here that require time and materials, there is no supplementary activity for this chapter.

Begin the chapter by discussing **Think On This...** from the end of chapter 3. Discuss the students' experiences with stress and ways they have dealt with stress. Be sure they include both positive and negative experiences with stress. Next, have the students suggest several things that they feel would be appropriate objectives for chapter 4 based on **Think On This...** at the end of chapter 3. Write these suggested objectives on the board/overhead. Then present the actual **Chapter Objectives** for chapter 4. Allow time to find the similarities and differences between their suggested objectives and the actual **Chapter Objectives**.

Present the **Working Vocabulary** words for the chapter one at a time, adding them to the lists from the previous chapters. The students should be able to recognize each word within the text.

Choose a student to read aloud "What Is Stress?" and "What Does Stress Do to Us?" on page 50. Begin a discussion about times when the students have felt stress. Ask the following question:

- *"Have any of you ever lost sleep due to a stressful situation? Can you describe the situation?"* (Answer: Answers will vary.)

Direct the students' attention to the long list of things that cause stress on pages 51 and 52. Have the students read through the list on their own for a few minutes. After they have had time to read a bit, ask the following questions:

- *"Does anyone think they can find a job that does not have any of the stresses mentioned here?"* (Answer: Probably not.)

- *"Can anyone think of a job that they believe has only one of the stresses mentioned here?"* (Answer: No job has only one or two stresses associated with it. It is best to learn to deal with stress in a constructive manner.)

Next, ask a student volunteer to read the part of Jill in the **Example** on page 52. Ask the following question:

- *"Can anyone think of other ways to make the stress of not having much money more bearable?"* (Answer: Trying to find things to do that don't cost money, such as bike riding, hiking, going on picnics, visiting museums, and so on.)

Ask a student to read aloud pages 53–54, "Stress and Relapse." Review the meaning of the word *relapse.* Then have the students associate the word with their lives. Ask them to think about what they might do if they experience a relapse. How can they combat these feelings? What do they really love to do that would take their mind off doing something that might draw them into a relapse?

Give each student an index card. Have them write at least three things they love to do that would take their mind off a poor behavior choice and prevent a relapse. Have them put these in their **purple folders.**

Assign the class to small groups. Have them complete **Think About It** on pages 54–55 together in the small groups. Then come together as a class to share some of the responses.

Ask the students to share some of the things that make them angry. Write these on the board/overhead. The following diagram shows an example of how to do this (see page 235 for a transparency master):

ANGRY—ANGER—MAD!	
THINGS THAT MAKE US ANGRY	THIS MAKES US ANGRY BECAUSE WE FEEL...
•	•
•	•
•	•

Then ask the students to describe why these things make them angry. Keep the diagram on the board/overhead while a student reads aloud "Stress and Anger" on page 55 and "What Causes Anger?" on pages 55–56. Ask the following question:

- *"How many of the items on page 54 and things you mentioned on the board/ overhead are related to the things that were discussed in the text on pages 55 and 56?"* (Answer: Answers will vary.)

Discuss ways the students have learned to handle anger. Write all these things on the board/overhead, both positive and negative. Use the following diagram as a guide (see page 236 for a transparency master):

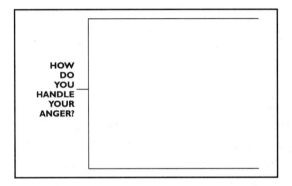

HOW
DO
YOU
HANDLE
YOUR
ANGER?

Then break the class into small groups. Give each group a piece of chart paper and a marker. Allow 10 minutes for each group to divide the suggestions about handling anger into three categories: MOST POSITIVE, PRETTY GOOD, and POOR CHOICES. Next, share the three-column charts with the class by posting them on the walls in the room. Take a few minutes to point out the differences between the charts.

Call on a student to read aloud "Handle Anger" on pages 57–58. Choose another volunteer to read the part of Sammy in the **Example** on page 58. Ask the following questions:

- *"How do you feel about channeling your anger? Do you think you can do this? Do you believe you can do this?"* (Answer: Answers will vary.)

- *"Can you think of some ways you can channel your anger? Write these in a space on your **purple folder** under the heading STOP ANGER NOW!*

Complete **Think About It** on pages 58–59 in small groups. Allow about 10 minutes for the groups to finish writing their answers. Share the responses as a class.

Direct the students' attention to "Relieve Stress" on pages 60–63. Have the students read through these items silently for a few minutes. Ask them to put a star beside those items that they feel they will be most likely to use in their daily lives as ways to relieve stress. They should put a question mark next to any item that seems odd to them and put an *x* next to any item they feel will not work for them in their lives.

When all the students have finished marking the list of items, break the class into small groups. Give each group a sheet of chart paper and a marker. Have them group the items on the pages in two ways, as shown in the following diagram (see page 237 for a transparency master):

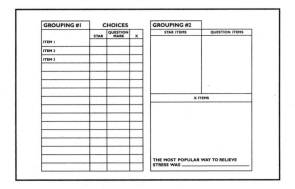

The first grouping should show how many students in the group marked each item with a star, a question mark, or an *x*. The second grouping will be a list of the items most frequently marked with each symbol, followed by the most popular way their group chose to relieve stress. Have each group share its results with the class.

Choose a student to read aloud the part of George in the **Example** on page 63. When the student has finished reading, ask the following question:

- *"Would anyone like to share some suggestions about things to think about that are pleasant enough to take your thoughts away from the stress you are feeling?"* (Answers will vary.)

Choose a student to read aloud page 64, "Look Closely at Work Pressures." Then break the class into small groups. Have them read pages 64–66 in the groups. Then give each group a sheet of paper. Have them rank the items on pages 64–66 in order from the one they think is the best suggestion to the one they feel is the suggestion they are least likely to use to avoid stress. Share these rankings with the entire class when finished. Have the students write their top three in the **Think About It** space on page 67.

Direct the class's attention to "Stress-Reduction Exercises" on pages 67–68. Go around the room and have each student read the instructions for one of the exercises. Then have the students perform the exercise in class. Continue this pattern until each exercise has been performed.

Call on a student to read aloud "Panic and Anxiety Attacks" on pages 69–70. When he is finished reading the section, ask the following questions:

- *"Describe what happens to someone who is experiencing a panic attack."* (Answer: Racing heart, sweating, dizziness, shortness of breath. They might think they are dying or losing their mind.)

- *"What will a panic attack not do to you?"* (Answer: Make you lose control, faint, or die.)

- *"How can you get through a panic attack?"* (Answer: Take long, slow, deep breaths and talk to yourself to get through the attack.)

Assign the section "Dealing with Burnout" on pages 70–71 to be read silently. When most of the students have finished reading, discuss the types of jobs that the students feel would most likely cause burnout. Be sure they mention jobs such as assembly-line work or factory jobs. Point out that factory jobs often pay well to compensate the workers for the repetitive nature of the job. Ask their opinion on the ideas for avoiding burnout. Discuss these subjects as a class.

Choose students to read "Reminder Questions to Ask Yourself about Stress" and "And Don't Forget..." on page 72. Give each student an index card to copy the questions, and have them put the card in their **purple folders.** This way, it will be close at hand when they really need it.

Select another student to read aloud the part of George in the **Example** on page 72. Emphasize the point that all of these things take *time.* Explain that they must take things one at a time and really enjoy them one at a time. They will get there!

Then have the students complete **Checkpoint** on pages 73–74. When they are finished, discuss the answers with the class.

Checkpoint Answers

1. See the list of things that cause stress on pages 51–52.

2. See the list of ways to relieve stress on pages 60–63.

3. See the list of ways to avoid stress on pages 64–66.

4. See the list of exercises on pages 67–68.

Think On This...

- What are some things that working and having a job offer you that you don't have right now?

- Are these things attractive to you?

- How will work fit into the rest of your life?

- Are you the type of person who will center your life around work, or will you have a job only because it is necessary in order to have money to live?

Think about the work that is attractive to you, and focus on the positive things it will provide in your life for years to come.

Chapter Five

The Big Picture

CHAPTER OBJECTIVES

1. To think again about what work has to offer.

2. To think about how work fits into the rest of your life.

Working Vocabulary

- **Satisfaction.** Being happy and content are signs of *satisfaction*.

- **Fulfillment.** The feeling of pleasure and contribution to the good of something or someone else is *fulfillment*.

Presentation Suggestions

Briefly discuss the similarities between **Think On This...** from the end of chapter 4 and the **Chapter Objectives** for chapter 5. Both are very straightforward.

Move on to present the **Working Vocabulary.** Discuss both words. Be sure the students understand the difference between the two words, because they do not mean the same thing. Add these words to the previous lists for display in the room. Take the time now to review the entire set of vocabulary words from chapter 1 through chapter 5.

Call on a student to read aloud page 76, "Job Satisfaction."

Choose a student to read aloud "The Payoff: You and Your Job" and the **Example** on page 77. When the student has finished reading these sections, ask the following questions:

- *"What do you think of Sammy? Are you prepared to face a world that has changed while you have been in prison?"* (Answer: Answers will vary.)

- *"Will you be able to face the people who are 'like you were'?"* (Answer: Answers will vary.)

Ask the students to read "The Rest of Your Life—When You're Not at Work" on page 78 on their own. Call on a student to read the part of Reggie in the **Example** on page 78. Discuss the ways the students think their prison experience will have changed their outlook on life after they are released from prison.

Assign the students to small groups to read and discuss "Good Times" on pages 78–79 and "Your Own Time" on pages 79–80. Choose a student to read aloud the part of Paul in the **Example** on page 80. Ask someone to read "Plan Your Free Time" at the bottom of page 80. When the reading has been completed, give each group a sheet of chart paper and a marker. Draw the following diagram on the board/overhead (see page 238 for a transparency master).

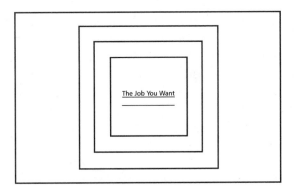

The Job You Want

Have the groups copy the diagram onto the chart paper. Then allow about five minutes for the group to think of productive ways to spend their free time once they are out in the world. Share these charts with the class. Post them in the room so that they are easily visible.

Then have the class complete pages 81–84 individually. Have the students pull out the **Free-Time Worksheet** and put it in their **purple folders**. Follow with **Activity #4** (see page 228).

Complete **Checkpoint** on page 85. Review the answers with the students.

Checkpoint Answers

1. Fulfillment and job satisfaction.

2. Answers will vary.

3. It is necessary to break the routine and have some fun and relaxation with family and friends.

Think On This...

Read aloud page 86, "Mendlin's Rules for the Road of Life." Explain that Ron Mendlin is one of the authors of these workbooks. He worked with parolees for more than 38 years, and he has helped nearly 600 people just like them find jobs. So he speaks from experience.

Ask the students to pull out their **purple folders** and find an empty space. Write each of the four areas of balance on the board/overhead:

- You must love at least one person.

- You must be loved.

- You must do work that is important to you.

- You must do something that is important to others.

When the students have completed copying these four areas onto their **purple folders**, ask, "Do you think that if you achieve these things, you really will have balance in your life? Explain why you think yes or no." (Answers will vary.)

Quick Quiz

Name: _____

Directions: *Find and circle the vocabulary words in the following puzzle.*

T	N	E	M	E	G	A	N	A	M	O	R	C	I	M
N	O	O	J	E	N	G	Q	Q	K	Y	O	Y	K	E
V	V	M	I	X	E	J	P	N	D	D	E	H	Y	D
G	R	K	I	T	F	S	C	C	O	Z	R	S	D	I
C	P	E	J	C	C	Y	P	N	T	E	A	T	C	T
Z	T	C	N	P	U	A	I	A	L	E	X	R	T	A
Y	M	P	P	F	U	L	F	I	L	L	M	E	N	T
M	B	G	V	B	J	Y	E	S	P	E	R	S	W	I
P	S	V	G	F	D	V	N	J	I	N	R	S	O	O
I	Y	Q	X	U	I	Q	W	S	I	T	D	T	A	N
Y	A	I	Y	N	R	V	B	W	V	P	A	Z	I	R
K	Z	B	G	B	J	B	C	S	O	Q	V	S	T	S

anxiety

fulfillment

meditation

micromanagement

relapse

relieving

satisfaction

stress

Quick Quiz Answer Key

T	N	E	M	E	G	A	N	A	M	O	R	C	I	M
N	O	O	J	E	N	G	Q	Q	K	Y	O	Y	K	E
V	V	M	I	X	E	J	P	N	D	D	E	H	Y	D
G	R	K	I	T	F	S	C	C	O	Z	R	S	D	I
C	P	E	J	C	C	Y	P	N	T	E	A	T	C	T
Z	T	C	N	P	U	A	I	A	L	E	X	R	T	A
Y	M	P	P	F	U	L	F	I	L	L	M	E	N	T
M	B	G	V	B	J	Y	E	S	P	E	R	S	W	I
P	S	V	G	F	D	V	N	J	I	N	R	S	O	O
I	Y	Q	X	U	I	Q	W	S	I	T	D	T	A	N
Y	A	I	Y	N	R	V	B	W	V	P	A	Z	I	R
K	Z	B	G	B	J	B	C	S	O	Q	V	S	T	S

Activity #1

Unwritten Rules Scripts

FORMAT: Pairs or small groups

TIME: 25–35 minutes

MATERIALS: Workbook page 14, pens/pencils, paper, index cards

1. Assign the students to groups or pairs.

2. Explain that the students will write a script and read it aloud.

3. The script should focus on one or two unwritten rules (refer to page 14) and will take place in the workplace. The "audience" (the rest of the class) will try to "pick up on" these unwritten rules as the script is read.

4. Before reading the script aloud, the group will give the instructor a card that has the unwritten rules they are portraying written on it.

5. The groups will read their scripts.

6. The class will try to identify the unwritten rules that the group tried to focus on.

7. Have fun!

Activity #2

To Do

FORMAT:	Individual
TIME:	20–25 minutes
MATERIALS:	Paper, pens/pencils, purple folder

1. Give the students two sheets of lined paper.

2. Explain that they should think of three good places they will be able to keep a "to-do" list. Have them write these places on the first piece of paper.

3. Tell the students to put a star next to the place they feel will work best for them.

4. On the second piece of paper, have the students create a list of at least 15 things they will need to do in their first week after leaving prison.

5. Have them put the list in their **purple folders.**

Activity #3

Conflict Compromise

FORMAT:	Small group
TIME:	15–20 minutes
MATERIALS:	Chart paper, pens/pencils, situation cards

1. Divide the class into small groups.

2. Explain that each group will pick a card from the stack. The card will have a basic workplace conflict described on it. The students will act out the conflict and a compromise that will ease the problem.

Situation Cards

Write each of these items on a separate card before class time:

A coworker is always nosing into everyone's business. Up until now it has been other people; now it's you. How do you tell him that you don't care for his actions?

One of your supervisors never speaks to anyone in a kind or constructive way. How can you stop his rudeness without being rude yourself?

Several of your coworkers never seem to be able to finish their work on time. Whenever the supervisor comes by to question why something has not been finished, they have an excuse. Now they are coming to you to cover for them. What do you do to stop this and make them take responsibility for their own actions?

People at your company gossip a lot. They seem to know all the personal details about everyone. They have asked you for information about a new person you work with, someone you are friends with. How can you derail their gossiping ways?

The copy machine is close to a worker's desk. This worker seems to believe he has the right to regulate the people who use the machine and know what they are copying. This person is always standing right by the copier. This bugs you. What can you do about it?

You are working in an office organized into cubicles. One of your coworkers is constantly barging into your cubicle, asking for assistance or information, or just to chat. You don't have time for this. Sometimes she even interrupts you when you are on the phone with a client. She never apologizes or considers that you have a job to do. How will you discuss this problem with her?

Activity #4

Getting the World on Your Side

FORMAT: Individual

TIME: 15–20 minutes

MATERIALS: Five index cards per student, pens/pencils

This is the same as **Activity #1** in *The "Double You": The Person You Are and the Person You Want to Be,* the first workbook in this series. If the class has used the complete series, it will be interesting for the students to see how their responses in this activity might have changed. It is worth doing this activity a second time.

1. Write these words in bold print on the board/overhead:

   RESPONSIBILITY, COURAGE, INSPIRATION, MOTIVATION, DEDICATION

2. Review the definitions of each word. (Refer to the **Working Vocabulary** list from chapter 1 of the first book in the series.)

3. Give each student five index cards.

4. Instruct the students to write the words in capital letters on the blank side of the cards, one word per card.

5. Have them number the cards in this order: 1. RESPONSIBILITY, 2. COURAGE, 3. INSPIRATION, 4. MOTIVATION, 5. DEDICATION.

6. On the reverse side of each card, the students will write a corresponding phrase and as many responses as they can think of.

   Card #1: I will take responsibility for my _____ .

   Card #2: I will have the courage to _____ .

   Card #3: My inspiration will come from _____ .

   Card #4: My motivation to succeed is _____ .

   Card #5: My dedication will show because I will _____ .

7. The students may share their responses with the class and perhaps share how their responses changed from the first time they completed this exercise.

8. The students should put the cards in their **purple folders.**

Comprehensive Quiz for Book 5

KEEPING YOUR JOB: SURVIVE AND SUCCEED IN A NEW JOB

Fill in the Blank

Directions: *Choose the correct word from the list to complete the sentence.*

Fulfillment   Gossip

Micromanagement   Negotiate

Relapse   Mentor

Meditation   Quota

Constructive comments   Honesty

1. Your boss tells you that you have a certain amount of work to complete in order to meet your _____ for promotion.

2. It could hurt your job success if you engage in rumors and _____ in the lunchroom.

3. Many people benefit from the use of quiet _____ to get away from everything.

4. Be careful not to _____ and return to bad habits from the past.

5. Jobs that make people feel they are contributing to the good of others offer _____ .

6. Employers look for workers who they feel tell the truth, showing a great deal of _____ .

7. Find a _____ , someone who will help you and guide you through life until you are on your feet.

8. Keep a positive outlook on your job by providing _____ about things that others do well while at work.

9. Giving a little and taking a little in order to solve a problem shows that you can _____ in response to a problem.

10. _____ occurs when your manager is too involved in the details of your work, instead of letting you handle things on your own.

True or False

Directions: *Decide whether the statement is true or false. If the statement is false, change it to make it true.*

1. Pressure that is put on you by something or someone else is stress.

2. Feeling displeased with a job shows that you are experiencing job satisfaction.

3. Making things worse than ever is a way of relieving stress in life.

4. Feeling that you are in control and happy shows that you do not have any anxiety.

5. Having manners shows that you know there is a standard of good behavior.

6. Being rude and loud when dealing with others is a sign that you are diplomatic.

7. Employers look for people they believe will show up and do their job well, because these kinds of people show dependability.

8. People who leave their desks messy and can't find important papers quickly are referred to as organized.

9. Prioritizing means putting things in order from most important to least important.

10. The image you project toward work, others, and yourself is your attitude.

11. "Supervisor" is another word for "boss."

12. A process is efficient if it takes a long time to complete and must be done many times to get it right.

13. Treating others the way you want them to treat you means that you have respect for them.

14. Not wanting to change your ideas or ways for anyone at any time shows an ability to be flexible.

Answer Key

Fill in the Blank

1. quota
2. gossip
3. meditation
4. relapse
5. fulfillment

6. honesty
7. mentor
8. constructive comments
9. negotiate
10. micromanagement

True or False

1. True

2. False; Feeling happy and fulfilled on your job shows that you are experiencing **job satisfaction.**

3. False; Taking things one at a time is a way of relieving stress in life.

4. True

5. True

6. False; Being polite and sensitive when dealing with others is a sign that you are **diplomatic.**

7. True

8. False; People whose desks are neat and can find important papers quickly are referred to as **organized.**

9. True

10. True

11. True

12. False; A process is **efficient** if it enables you to get something done quickly and with less effort.

13. True

14. False; Being willing to adapt your ideas or plans shows an ability to be **flexible.**

ATTACK THE PROBLEM, NOT THE PERSON!

CONFLICTS PRODUCE...

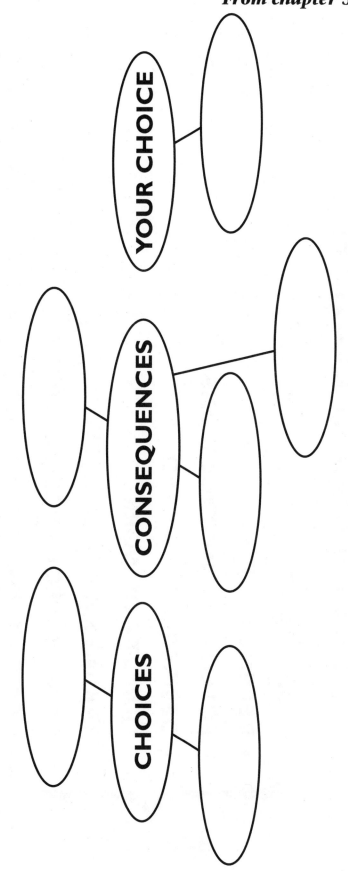

YOUR CHOICE

CONSEQUENCES

CHOICES

SUPERVISORS LOOK FOR

- WORK HABITS
- DEPENDABILITY
- FOLLOWING INSTRUCTIONS
- DESIRE TO GET AHEAD
- QUALITY OF WORK
- TAKING RESPONSIBILITY
- CONCERN FOR PRODUCTIVITY
- GOOD ATTITUDES TOWARD COMPANY AND EMPLOYER
- ABILITY TO SPEAK AND WRITE CLEARLY AND EFFECTIVELY
- ABILITY TO READ AND USE PRINTED INSTRUCTIONS

ATTITUDE

© 2000 • JIST Works • Indianapolis

From chapter 4, page 213

ANGRY—ANGER—MAD!

THINGS THAT MAKE US ANGRY	THIS MAKES US ANGRY BECAUSE WE FEEL...
*	*
*	*
*	*

From chapter 4, page 214

HOW
DO
YOU
HANDLE
YOUR
ANGER?

GROUPING #2

STAR ITEMS	QUESTION ITEMS

X ITEMS

THE MOST POPULAR WAY TO RELIEVE STRESS WAS _____

GROUPING #1

CHOICES

	STAR	QUESTION MARK	X
ITEM 1			
ITEM 2			
ITEM 3			

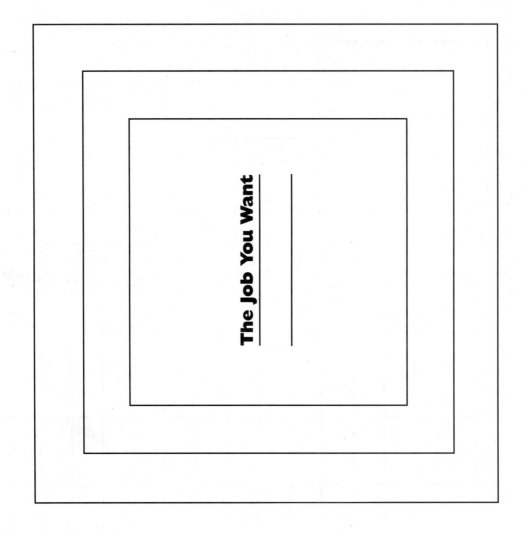

The Job You Want